THE DARK NIGHT
OF THE SOUL

THE DARK NIGHT
OF THE SOUL

ST. JOHN OF THE CROSS

TRANSLATED BY
GABRIELA CUNNINGHAME GRAHAM

INTRODUCTION BY
MARGARET KIM PETERSON

BARNES & NOBLE

NEW YORK

**THE BARNES & NOBLE
LIBRARY OF ESSENTIAL READING**

Introduction and Suggested Reading
© 2005 by Barnes & Noble, Inc.

Originally published in 1618

This 2005 edition published by Barnes & Noble, Inc.

Barnes & Noble, Inc.
122 Fifth Avenue
New York, NY 10011

ISBN: 978-0-7607-6587-6

Printed and bound in the United States of America

7 9 10 8 6

Contents

INTRODUCTION

IN *THE DARK NIGHT OF THE SOUL* THE SIXTEENTH-CENTURY SPANISH mystic St. John of the Cross describes the purification, or "night," that the human soul must experience as God's gift if it is to enter into loving union with God in this life. This loving union is the goal of the mystical life, a spiritual path that seeks not simply a right intellectual knowledge of God and the things of God, nor simply a moral likeness to God, but a relationship with God in which all that is not God is rigorously and systematically set aside and the mystery that is God's being is encountered directly by the human person. *The Dark Night of the Soul* is cast in the form of a commentary on John's poem of the same name, for, in addition to being a mystic, John was both a theologian and a poet. The book is thus a theological exposition of a mystical poem; in it, John reflects doctrinally and pastorally on his own mystical experience and that of the many others whom he had served as spiritual director and confessor. It is this combination of personal, pastoral, and academic wisdom that has made *The Dark Night of the Soul* an enduring classic in the literature of Christian spirituality. It is a book to which generations of readers, both lay and religious, have turned as they have sought to experience on earth the kind of intimacy with God that will characterize the lives of the blessed in heaven.

St. John of the Cross was a central figure in the renewal and reform of sixteenth-century Spanish religious life, particularly with respect to the Carmelite religious order, of which he was a member. John was born in 1542 in Fontiveros, Spain, and entered the Carmelite monastery in Medina del Campo when he was twenty-one. In 1567 he met Teresa of Avila, who was already much engaged in reforming the religious life of Carmelite nuns and who was looking for men to assist her in extending the reform to men of the order. John spent the rest of his life involved in the leadership of the reformed, or "discalced," branch of the Carmelites. The progress of the reform was anything but smooth, and at one point John was actually imprisoned for the better part of a year by members of the non-reformed branch of the order. When John escaped from prison, he did so with a notebook containing poetry written during his confinement. It was these poems, together with others written subsequently, that became the basis of John's prose treatises, including *The Dark Night of the Soul.* John's own "dark night" was thus not only the night of mystical contemplation and negation, but the night of imprisonment and physical suffering, of external circumstances that, John believed, God may work through to accomplish His purposes in the soul.

The Carmelite movement, in whose reform John was so intimately involved, had itself originated in an earlier period of reform, namely the *Vita Apostolica* movement of the twelfth and thirteenth centuries. The *Vita Apostolica,* or apostolic life, was the name given by devout men and women to their efforts to imitate in specific detail the lives of Christ and the apostles. Central elements of the apostolic life included a radical poverty like that spoken of in the gospels (no money, no shoes, no spare tunic; cf. Mt. 10:9–10) and a devotion to prayerful contemplation on the mystery of Christ. The apostolic life was pursued in Italy by the disciples of St. Francis and by other groups of lay hermits. In the wake of the First Crusade the apostolic life spread to the Holy Land, where numbers of hermits took up residence in sites associated with the life of Christ and with Old Testament patriarchs and prophets. Toward the end of the twelfth century, many of these hermits began to cluster on Mount Carmel, where, taking Elijah as their model, they practiced an ascetic and contemplative life that they believed stood in direct succession to that of the prophet.

As the political instability of the Crusader kingdom grew, the hermits of Mount Carmel began in the thirteenth century to migrate to the West, taking with them the common Rule that they had received from Albert, the Latin patriarch of Jerusalem. This had stipulated, among other things, that each hermit have his own cave-dwelling in which he could remain night and day, engaged in continual prayer. But individual cave-dwellings were difficult to come by in Europe; nor could other properly remote hermitages easily be found. The Carmelites thus requested of the Pope that their Rule be amended to allow them to settle in cities, which permission was granted in 1247 by Innocent IV. This began a century-long transition by which the Carmelites ceased to be hermits (living remote and solitary lives of contemplation) and became mendicants (living in cities and engaging in ministries of teaching and preaching), as the followers of St. Francis and others had done before them. These changes in the Carmelite vocation, along with the social and political upheavals of the fourteenth century (including, for example, the Black Death), led to more changes in the Rule, whose original insistence on abstinence (that is, from meat), extended fasts, and silence—all disciplines intended to strengthen the spiritual life by weakening attachment to worldly pleasures—was repeatedly attenuated. By the fifteenth century, the religious life of the Carmelites had suffered significant decline.

Two related but distinct movements—which in Spain owed much to the general climate of religious reform and renewal encouraged by the Catholic monarchs Ferdinand and Isabella—were to reverse this trend, and bring reform and renewal to the order. One was the desire, among reform-minded Carmelites, to return to observance of the primitive rule of the order, with particular stress laid on poverty and penitential practice (both of which were often symbolized by going barefoot) and the contemplative life. The other was the development of practices of prayer that, while not rejecting such practices as communal, vocal prayer, or the recitation of the psalter, stressed interiority and the role of contemplation as essential means of fostering a loving union with God in this life. Both movements came to spectacular flower in the life and work of St. Teresa of Avila, and then in that of her younger disciple and colleague, St. John of the Cross.

St. Teresa of Avila had been born in 1515 to a wealthy and pious family in Toledo, and in 1535 entered the Carmelite monastery at Avila. She had learned about contemplative prayer early in her

religious life but had found herself frustrated in her efforts to persevere in it. Through a process that included extensive reading of
spiritual writers and conversation with many confessors and theological advisors, Teresa found herself drawn into a mystical life that
overflowed into the reform of the Carmelite order and the renewal
of Carmelite spirituality. In 1562 she founded the first convent of
"discalced" (barefoot) Carmelite nuns, and went on to found twenty
more before her death in 1582. These convents were marked by an
atmosphere of solitude and silence and included several hours each
day that were dedicated to mental (as opposed to vocal or communal)
prayer. Teresa wrote several books for the instruction of her discalced
nuns that have become enduring spiritual classics; among them are
The Way of Perfection and *The Interior Castle.*

The Teresian reform had been underway for five years when
Teresa and John first met. She was fifty-two; he was twenty-five, newly
ordained to the priesthood, and desiring a more fully contemplative
life than was available to him in the (calced) Carmelite monastery
of which he was a member. For Teresa, who had recently received
permission from the prior general of the order to found two houses
of discalced friars, John was an answer to prayer, albeit in unexpected
form: John was so short in stature that Teresa is reported to have said,
"Lord, I asked you for a monk, and you sent me half of one." In
November of 1568, John became one of the first two discalced friars
of the Carmelite order. Antonio de Heredia, the former prior of
Medina, was superior of the house; John was the novice master, beginning what would become a lifelong work in spiritual direction. When
three years later, in 1571, Teresa was appointed prioress of the
Incarnation monastery in Avila, she invited John to be the spiritual
director there for her nuns and for herself, a position he occupied
for five years. Teresa's and John's collaboration during those years
was such that, according to John's biographer E. W. T. Dicken, each
is most profitably read together with the other. John was a poet with a
theologian's education and discipline; Teresa wrote from a depth and
breadth of personal experience and relationship. "Together they present us with an overall perspective view of the theology and practice of

the spiritual life which, for Christians of the Western Church, constitutes the almost indispensable key to all serious study of the subject in both earlier and later writers."

During John's years as chaplain and confessor to the nuns of the Incarnation, conflicts arose within the order about to whom the office properly belonged. John's tenure ended abruptly in 1577, when friars belonging to a rival group kidnapped John and imprisoned him at the Carmelite monastery of Toledo. He remained there for nine months, in a room six feet by nine feet, with one two-inch-wide window high in the wall and little in the way of either food or clothing. In the midst of this "dark night" of abandonment and privation, John turned for solace to poetry, composing poems now esteemed as among the greatest lyric poetry in Spanish literature. In these poems, John sought to give expression to some of the seeming incompatibilities of his experience and the synthesis they found in God: darkness and light, emptiness and fullness, desire and fulfillment, detachment and union, nothingness and the divine essence.

John escaped from prison in August 1578 and found refuge with a monastery of Teresian nuns in Toledo. His allies in the order soon appointed him vicar of El Calvario, a monastery in an area of southern Spain remote enough that he would be unlikely to be kidnapped again. Two years later, the conflicts over jurisdiction were resolved when the discalced friars and nuns were allowed to form a new province and govern themselves. By this time, John had already left El Calvario for Baeza, where he was rector of a new college for discalced students in the south. In 1582 he moved to Granada, where he held various high administrative posts in the order while continuing to serve as spiritual director for various groups of friars and nuns. It was in the context of this work that he wrote his prose treatises on spirituality, all of which were composed as commentaries on his previously written poems. During these years he traveled a great deal, visiting houses of friars and nuns and founding seven new monasteries. He moved in university circles, and was known and respected as an expert in Scripture, theology, and spirituality. In his later years, however, he again became involved in conflict within the order.

He had been serving as councilor to the vicar general, Nicolás Doria, in Castile for several years when in 1591 he was sent away to the remote monastery of La Peñuela. There he fell ill, and after months of suffering, both from sickness and from inadequate medical care, he died in the nearby town of Ubeda on December 14, 1591.

John left only a modest corpus of written work: some counsels and maxims, a dozen or so poems, a few short letters, and four book-length commentaries on four of his poems, together amounting to perhaps one thousand pages. He was not in the first instance a writer; he was a contemplative and a spiritual director, turning to poetry as an expression of the depths and heights of his mystical experience, and to prose when the friars and nuns under his direction read his poems and asked him to explain what he meant. Both John's poetry and his prose are characterized by lyrical, symbolic language, which inspired mystics but made theologians nervous. In the Western theological tradition of which John was a part, symbolic language was restricted to devotional literature, while theology was written using conceptual language. The symbol of the "dark night," which is so central to John, thus seemed quite out of place to many of his contemporaries when they encountered it in his theological treatises.

This nervousness was amplified in the generally suspicious religious climate that characterized the Spain of John's day. Half a century before, Ferdinand and Isabella's encouragement of religious reform had included the imposition of orthodoxy as a means of ensuring political and social stability in a recently re-unified country. The means of imposing this orthodoxy, the Spanish Inquisition, was in full swing by the middle of the sixteenth century, publishing lists of forbidden books, interviewing and silencing anyone whose teaching seemed problematic in anyway, and, in view of the Protestant reformation that was going on elsewhere in Europe, giving particular attention to anything that smacked of "Lutheranism." The mysticism of John of the Cross had nothing to do with Lutheranism, but its emphasis on the relation of the individual soul to God, combined with its unusual use of language and imagery, was enough to give a lot of people pause. As a result, the first printed edition of John's works, which appeared in 1618, was characterized by numerous editorial changes—both deletions and additions—that were meant to deflect suspicions of false teaching. Most of these editorial changes were carried over into subsequent editions, until in the early twentieth century a revival of interest in early Carmelite spirituality led to the production of critical editions based on the manuscripts. Free of both the suspicion and neglect that marked his legacy for several hundred years, John of the Cross is now regarded as one of Spain's greatest poets and one of the Church's greatest mystical theologians. He was acknowledged as a Doctor of the Church (that is, a notably authoritative teacher) in 1926. Teresa of Avila was similarly recognized in 1970, the first woman ever to be a Doctor of the Church. (One other woman has since been given this title, and she also was a Carmelite: St. Thérèse of Lisieux.)

John's four prose treatises include, in addition to *The Dark Night of the Soul*, *The Ascent of Mount Carmel*, *The Spiritual Canticle*, and *The Living Flame of Love*. Each is a commentary on a poem of the same name, except for *The Ascent of Mount Carmel* and *The Dark Night of the Soul*, which both comment on the same poem, *The Dark Night*. John employs the symbol of the "dark night" as a general term denoting the whole discipline of privation or renunciation, from the beginning of the spiritual life to its end. This discipline has two aspects: the active night of voluntary self-discipline, and the passive night of God-given privation (whether this be experienced purely spiritually or through external circumstances as well). The purpose of both the active night and the passive night is to detach the soul from its love for all that is not God, so that it can enter into an undistracted and thus genuine union with God in love. The Christian mystical practice of detachment is thus founded neither on a denial of the reality of that-which-is-not-God (such things have real existence as God's creatures) nor on a denial of the goodness of such things (they are God's *good* creatures), but on an insistence that however real or good a creature may be, it is not God, and cannot and should not be the object of the most intimate love of which a human being is capable. That love is reserved for God alone, and while a loving union with God is not something a human being can work his or her way into, the privative disciplines of the contemplative life are intended to fit the soul to receive this gift, should God graciously choose to bestow it.

Although the *Ascent* and the *Dark Night* have come down in the tradition as separate books, they are intimately connected with each other. The *Ascent* corresponds roughly to the "active night of the soul" and the *Dark Night* to the "passive night of the soul." Two other elements complete this complex work: the eight stanzas of the poem *The Dark Night*, which was written during John's time at El Calvario (1578–79) following his escape from prison, and a sketch by John of Mount Carmel, the "mount of perfection," which serves as a visual summary of the mystical experience that John expresses in his poem and explains in his commentary. This image of Mount Carmel, which obviously hearkens back to the origins of the Carmelite order and its particular devotion to Elijah, was intended by John to be a part of his commentary, as he shows when he refers to "the drawing at the beginning of the book." The treatise *The Ascent of Mount Carmel* takes its title from the sketch; *The Dark Night of the Soul* takes its title from the poem.

The Dark Night of the Soul is not a commentary in the usual sense of the term, in that the text upon which John is ostensibly commenting is a poem of eight stanzas, but he comments only on the first two stanzas (explaining the first stanza twice), barely mentions the third, and then ends the book. As John's purpose in writing was to offer a theological exposition and interpretation of some of the imagery of the poem, perhaps he felt at this point that he had done all he could, and thus he wrote no more. The book describes the passive night of the soul, which John further subdivides into the passive night of the senses and the passive night of the spirit. Numbering introduced by the first editor of John's works identifies these sections as two books, the first with fourteen chapters and the second with twenty-five chapters. Throughout the work, John retains a dual perspective on his subject: the description of mystical experience contained in the poem and the theological analysis of that experience contained in the book. Even at its most technically theological, however, John's exposition is never doctrinaire. It is informed at every point, not only by his own experience, but by his attention to the experiences of countless others whose spiritual development he had been privileged to observe as they made their own ascents into the mysterious darkness that is God's love.

That juxtaposition of darkness and love, so central to all John's works, but especially *The Dark Night of the Soul*, is deeply expressive of the paradox central to the Christian faith: that in the cross of Christ, in that abyss of suffering and degradation, is the ultimate expression of the love of an all-powerful and all-merciful God. It is thus perhaps no surprise that John's writings have proven powerfully attractive to persons grappling with terrible evils and attempting at the same time to experience and respond to them within the context of their Christian faith. T. S. Eliot, in the second of his *Four Quartets*, written just after the outbreak of the second World War, invokes the negative spirituality of John of the Cross: "be still, and let the dark come upon you." His aim was evidently not the nihilistic one of embracing darkness for itself, but the Christian one of embracing the light that can come only after the darkness is acknowledged for what it is: for, Eliot goes on to say, one day "the darkness shall be the light, and the stillness the dancing."

In the wake of the war, the Trappist monk Thomas Merton likewise looked to St. John of the Cross as a teacher and a guide. Merton was a contemplative monk who was also deeply involved in the civil rights and peace movements. His social involvements were, Merton believed, perfectly congruent with a Christian life of prayer. The very negativity of contemplative prayer, its rigorous insistence on the rejection of all that is not God, gives it a "uselessness" that purifies it from the selfishness and manipulativeness that too often characterize petitionary prayer. It is when prayer is most contemplative that it can issue truly charitable action, says Merton. "There is no contradiction between action and contemplation when Christian apostolic activity is raised to the level of pure charity. On that level, action and contemplation are fused into one activity by the love of God and of our brother in Christ."

St. John of the Cross would have agreed. The Christian mystic enters into the darkness of contemplation not to avoid the messiness of the world and its evils, but in order to encounter both God and God's world on God's terms, in the midst of the darkness in which God's light is paradoxically hid. Only so can men and women of faith be formed in the perfect charity for which they were made. As John himself notes, "at the end of the day, the subject of examination will be love."

Margaret Kim Peterson is Theologian in Residence at the First Presbyterian Church at Norristown, Pennsylvania. She teaches theology at Eastern University in St. Davids, Pennsylvania.

BOOK I

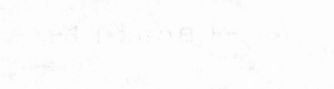

THE DARK NIGHT OF THE SOUL
AND DECLARATION OF THE SONGS

WHICH EMBRACES THE ROAD TO THE PERFECT UNION OF LOVE WITH
God, as far as may be in this Life; and the admirable properties of the
soul which has reached thereto.

ARGUMENT

In this book are first set down all the songs which are to be declared;
and then each one is separately expounded, setting the song before
the gloss, and afterwards proceeding to shew the meaning of each line
one by one, placing the line first.

In the first two songs are described the effects of the two Spiritual
purgations of the Sensitive part of man and the Spiritual. In the
following six are described various and admirable effects of Spiritual
Illumination and Union of Love with God.

SONG OF THE SOUL

Into the darkness of the night
With heart ache kindled into love,
Oh blessed chance!
I stole me forth unseen,
My house being wrapped in sleep.

Into the darkness, and yet safe
By secret stair and in disguise,
Oh gladsome hap!

In darkness, and in secret I crept forth,
My house being wrapt in sleep.

Into the happy night
In secret, seen of none,
Nor saw I ought,
Without, or other light or guide,
Save that which in my heart did burn.

This fire it was that guided me
More certainly than midday sun,
Where he did wait,
He that I knew imprinted on my heart,
In place, where none appeared.

Oh Night, that led me, guiding night,
Oh Night far sweeter than the Dawn;
Oh Night, that did so then unite
The Loved with his Beloved,
Transforming Lover in Beloved.

On my blossoming breast,
Alone for him entire was kept,
He fell asleep,
Whilst I caressed,
And fanned him with the cedar fan.

The breeze from forth the battlements,
As then it tossed his hair about,
With his fair hand
He touched me lightly on the neck,
And reft me of my senses in a swoon.

I lay quite still, all mem'ry lost,
I leaned my face upon my Loved One's breast;
I knew no more, in sweet abandonment
I cast away my care,
And left it all forgot amidst the lilies fair.

EXPOSITION OF THE PURPORT OF THE SONGS

Before we enter on the interpretation of these songs, it behoves us here to know that they are the utterances of the Soul which has arrived at perfection, which is the Union of Love with God, she having, at last, passed through rigorous trials and conflicts, by spiritual practice of the narrow road which leads to life eternal, as saith our Savior in the Gospel, which must, as a rule, be traversed by the soul if she is to arrive at this sublime and divine Union with God: *Quam angusta porta, et arcta via est, quæ ducit ad vitam: et pauci sunt, qui inveniunt eam.*[1] The which, inasmuch as it is so strait, and they so few that enter thereon (as the Lord Himself likewise says), the soul counts it for great happiness and good fortune that she has won therethrough to the aforesaid perfection of love, like as she sings in this her first Song, where, with exceeding propriety, she likens this strait and narrow road to a darksome night, as is shewn further on in the lines of the aforesaid Song. The soul, then, rejoicing in the successful issue of her journey from this narrow road whence she has derived so great a treasure, proceeds to unburthen herself in manner following.

Wherein the Night of the Senses is Treated of

SONG THE FIRST

Into the darkness of an obscure Night
Burning with passionate longing for my love,
Oh gladsome chance!
I sallied forth with none to note,
My house being now asleep.

DECLARATION

IN THIS FIRST SONG THE SOUL RELATES THE MODE AND MANNER SHE pursued as regards her emotions and sensations, when she set forth from herself and all things, dying with unfeigned mortification to herself and them, so as to attain at last a sweet and pleasant life of love in God; and she says that this going forth from herself and all things, was "In a dark night," whereby she means purgative contemplation, as shall afterwards be said; the which causes in the soul the negation of herself and of everything.

And this outgoing, she says here, she was enabled to effect by the strength and ardor given to her for this purpose by the love of her Spouse in the aforesaid obscure contemplation. Wherein she extols the good fortune she had on her journey to God through this dark night, with so prosperous an issue, that none of the three enemies, which are the world, the flesh, and the devil (who ever obstruct this road), had power to stop her, so effectually did this said night of purificative contemplation put to sleep and deaden by its contrary motions every passion and appetite in the house of her sensuality.

THE FIRST LINE IS SET DOWN, AND THE IMPERFECTIONS OF BEGINNERS ARE COMMENCED TO BE TREATED OF

IN A DARK NIGHT

Souls begin to enter this dark night when God proceeds to lead them from the state of beginners, proper to those who meditate on the spiritual road, and begins to set them in that of the progressives, which is, at length, that of the contemplatives, to the end, that passing through this state, they may reach that of the perfect, which is the Divine union of the Soul with God. Therefore, so that we may the better understand and set forth what night this is where through the soul passes, and for what cause God places her therein, we must here first touch upon some propensities of beginners, so that they may know the weakness of their state, and pluck up courage, and desire that God may set them in this night, wherein the soul is strengthened and confirmed in virtue and made ready for the inestimable delights of the love of God. And even though we dwell somewhat thereon, it will not be more than suffices in order adequately to treat, further on, of this dark night. We must then know that, after the soul resolutely converts herself to serve God, God generally sets to work to educate her spiritually and to regale her, as does a loving mother her tender child, whom she warms at the heat of her breast, and rears with sweet milk and soft and delicate food and bears about in her arms and cherishes; but, by degrees, as it waxes in growth, the mother begins to wean it and hiding from it her soft breast, anoints it with bitter aloes, and putting the infant from her arms, teaches it to walk with its feet, to the end that, losing its childish ways, it may become used to greater and more real things.

The loving mother of the grace of God, as soon as she regenerates the soul, by inspiring her with renewed ardor and fervency to serve God, does likewise. For, without any effort of her own, she causes her to find sweet and pleasant spiritual milk in everything belonging to God and great delight in spiritual exercises, because now God gives her his breast of tender love, like as she were a child. Wherefore she ciphers her delight in passing long hours in prayer, and, perchance, whole nights; her pleasures are penances, her enjoyments fasts, her comfort to partake of the Sacraments and discourse of Divine matters. In which things, although the spiritually minded assist with great efficacy and assiduousness and use to treat with the utmost solicitude, yet, speaking in the spiritual sense, they conduct themselves therein most weakly and imperfectly. For, as they are moved to these things and spiritual exercises by the comfort and relish they find therein; and as, likewise, they have not acquired sufficient skill, by the practice of stubborn wrestling with virtue, they are, in these their spiritual works, subject to many faults and imperfections; because, in short, each one acts conformably to that degree of perfection he possesses, and as they have had no opportunity to acquire the aforesaid rigorous habits they must, perforce, like children, act weakly. The which, in order to make clearer, as also the weakness wherewith these beginners advance in virtue, in respect of what, with the aforesaid relish, they easily accomplish, we shall note as we go on under the seven capital vices, setting forth some of the many imperfections they incur as regards each. Wherein it will be clearly seen how their performances are little better than child's play. And it shall also be seen how great are the treasures which the dark night, whereof we are about to treat, brings with it; since it cleanses and purifies the soul from all her imperfections.

OF SOME SPIRITUAL IMPERFECTIONS WHICH BESET BEGINNERS AS REGARDS PRIDE

When these beginners feel in themselves such fervency and activity in devout exercises, this very prosperity (although it is true that of themselves holy things beget humility), produces in them, by reason of their imperfection, a certain ramification of secret pride, whence they begin to view their works and themselves with a certain sort of complacency. And hence, also, springs an exceeding vain desire to speak of spiritual things with others, and even, at times, to teach them rather than to learn, and in their hearts they condemn others if they do not perceive in them the sort of devotion that chimes in with their own tastes, and occasionally, even, they give vent to their opinions in words, being like in this to the Pharisee who boasted of the things he did, and despised the Publican. Ofttimes does the devil increase in them the fervor and desire to perform these and other deeds on purpose that their pride and presumption shall wax greater. For well does the devil know that all these actions and virtues they perform are not only worthless to them, but are rather turned into vices. And to such a length do some of these people get that they would fain none were found good save themselves; and so, by word and deed, when they meet with such a one, they condemn and slander him: seeing the mote in their neighbor's eye and not considering the beam in their own, they strain at his gnat and gulp down their own camel: *Quid autem vides festucam in oculo fratris tui, et trabem in oculo tuo non vides?*[1]

Sometimes also, when their spiritual masters, such as confessors and superiors, approve not their spirit and mode of proceeding (for they hanker after their applause and esteem), they decide that they understand not their spirit and are not spiritually minded, since they do not approve of, and agree with, their own. And therefore they desire, and do their best, to consult with some other, who squares with their taste; for, as a rule, they like to discuss their spirit with those whom, they have a notion, are sure to praise and make much of it. They fly, as from death itself, from those who, to put them on a surer road, make light thereof, and sometimes, even, bear them ill will. Presuming greatly in themselves, their wont is to propose much and do little. At times they are eager that their companions should witness their spirit and devotion: and to this end they make exterior displays of motions, sighs, and other outward shows, and at times are wont to have this or the other ecstasy in public rather than in secret, in all which the devil lends a helping hand; and that others should see that they so ardently covet, fills them with complacency. Many seek to become favorites with their confessors, and, hence, expose themselves to a thousand envies and disquietudes. They take shame to confess their naked sins lest their confessor shall think less of them, and proceed to lend them another sort of color so that they shall not seem so bad, which is rather to excuse themselves than to accuse. At times they look out for another confessor to confess their sins to, so that their own shall think they have none at all, but that all is well; and thus, they are always pleased to confess to him all that is good, and at times, in such terms as to make it seem even better than it is (at least, their wish is that he should think so); whereas it would argue more humility on their part, as we shall presently show, to make nought thereof, and be solicitous that neither he nor anyone else should attach the slightest importance thereto. Some of these, also, think lightly of their faults, and at other times are saddened over much when they see themselves fall therein, thinking that, at length, they were saints, and wax wrath against themselves with great impatience, which is another exceeding imperfection. Often they plead anxiously with God to deliver them from their imperfections and failings, more for the sake of being themselves spared the molestation thereof and to be at peace, than for the sake of God, not considering that if He freed them therefrom, they would, perchance, wax still haughtier in their pride. They hate to praise others, and delight in being praised, and at times they claim it as a right; wherein they are like to the foolish virgins who, having allowed their lamps to become extinguished, go forth to seek for oil from their neighbors. *Date nobis de oleo vestro, quia lampades nostre extinguuntur.*[2]

From these imperfections, some get to many others in an extreme degree, and to great evil therein. But some are subject to fewer imperfections and others to more, and there are scarce any of these beginners who, in the season of their fervors, fall not into somewhat of this nature. But they who, in this season walk in perfection, proceed in a very different manner and in a very different frame of spirit; for they make progress in, and build upon, the foundation of humility, not only holding their own deeds in nought, but with the exceeding small satisfaction they have of themselves, they hold all others incomparably better than themselves and are wont to bear them a holy envy, desiring to serve God, as they do. For the greater their fervor, the more are the works they perform and take delight in, and, as they walk in humbleness, the more do they perceive how greatly God deserves of them and how little is the utmost they do for Him, and so the more they do, the less they are satisfied. For so great is that which for very charity and love they were fain do for Him, that all they do, they count as nought; and so strongly does this poignancy of love urge and absorb them, that they never notice what others do or do not do; or if they notice, it is with the absolute conviction, as I say, that everyone else is far better than they are themselves. Whence, holding themselves in no esteem, they are solicitous that others should do likewise, and make little of and despise their own doings. And, furthermore, even though others were fain to praise and make much of them, they can in no way be brought to believe it, and it appears to them passing strange that such praises should be said of them.

These, with great tranquility and humility, are exceeding anxious to learn from whosoever can direct them; most opposite indeed to the behavior of those we have spoken of above, who were fain to teach everything, and, even when it seems that others would teach them somewhat, they take the words out of their mouth as if, already, there were nothing left for them to learn. But these are very far from seeking to pose as masters of anyone. They are exceeding quick to learn and to take another road from that they are on, if so they should be bidden, for never do they think that they hit the mark in anything. In the praises of others they rejoice: their only sorrow is that they serve not God as they do. They do not hanker to talk about their experiences, because so lightly do they hold them, that they take shame even to speak of them to their spiritual masters, thinking they are unworthy to be mentioned. They are more eager to recount their failings and their sins, or to convince their confessors that they are not virtues; and therefore, they are more inclined to discuss their soul with him who sets the least store upon their experiences and spirit. The which is a propensity of a simple, pure, and unfeigned spirit, and most agreeable to God. For as the wise spirit of God takes up its abode in these humble souls, it at once moves and inclines them to guard their treasures inwardly in secret, and to cast out evil. Because, together with all other virtues, God gives this grace to the humble, just as He denies it to the proud.

To whomsoever serves God, these will give their heart's blood, and will do all in their power to help him to do Him service. When they fall into imperfections they bear themselves with humility and pliability of spirit and loving fear of God and hoping in Him. But souls which, from the first, travel in such a sort of perfection as is this (I mean as has been mentioned), are very few, and indeed, so exceeding few that we might well rejoice if they fall not into the opposite extreme. For which reason, as we shall afterwards show, God sets those He wishes to purify of all these imperfections, in the dark night, so as to bring them on still further.

OF THE IMPERFECTIONS WHICH SOME BEGINNERS ARE WONT TO ENTERTAIN
AS TO THE SECOND CAPITAL VICE, WHICH, TO SPEAK SPIRITUALLY, IS AVARICE

At times, also, many of these beginners are subject to great spiritual avarice. For rarely shall you see them content with the spirit God gives them, but most disconsolate and querulous because they find not in spiritual things the comfort they desire. Many are never done of listening to advice and spiritual counsel, and of getting and reading many books which treat thereof, and so, engaged in this, and not in practical deeds, time slips by and leaves them without the mortification and perfection of interior poverty of spirit which is required of them. For, over and above this, they load themselves up with images, rosaries, and crosses exceeding handsome and valuable; now they reject some and take up another; now they barter them for something else; now they undo their bargains; at one moment they want them of this fashion, at the end of that, taking a fancy to this rather than the other, inasmuch as it is rarer or more costly.

Then shall you see others adorned with Agnus Dei, and reliquaries and relics, like children with trinkets. Wherein I condemn the predilection of the heart, and the clinging to the fashion, variety, and rarity of these things; inasmuch as it is utterly opposed to poverty of spirit, which is fixed solely on the essence of devotion, making use of that only which suffices thereto, this other sort of variety and rareness being, to them, a weariness of the flesh; for true devotion must spring from the heart, and fix its eyes, to the exclusion of all else, on the truth and substance underlying the outward shews of spiritual things, and anything besides is attachment and a property of imperfection, for if we would go forward to the state of perfection, it is necessary to make an end of such a tendency. I knew a person who, for more than ten years, made use of a cross rudely fashioned from a branch which had been consecrated, held together by a crooked pin, and had never forsaken it, and bore it about him constantly until I took it away; and this person was far from being a fool and weak of intellect. And I knew another, who used a rosary made of bones of fishes' spines, whose devotion, it is certain, was not less pure, nor less highly prized by, and acceptable to, God; since it is clearly seen that the value thereof had nought to do with the fashion and costliness of such things as these. Those who start, then, well grounded in these principles, will not cling to visible instruments nor load themselves up therewith, nor will it matter to them one jot to know more than what is essential to performance; for they fix their eyes solely on being well with God, in pleasing Him, and are greedy for this alone. Wherefore they give away most liberally and freely whatsoever they possess, and their delight is to know that they are left without it for the sake of God and neighborly charity, ordering all things according to the laws of this virtue. For, as I say, they keep their eyes set solely on the real things of perfection, on pleasing God, and not themselves, in anything. But not from these imperfections, nor from any others, can the soul purify herself completely, until God sets her in the passive purgation of that dark night we shall presently speak of. But it behoves the soul, in so far as she is able, to do all she can to purge and perfect herself, so as to deserve that God shall place her under this Divine Regimen, where the soul is healed of all she does not succeed in curing of herself. For howsoever the soul may assist thereto, she cannot, for all her industry, actively purify herself as to be fit, in the slightest degree, for the Divine union of perfection of love with God, were He not to put forth His hand and purge her in this, for her, so dark a fire, still to be described.

OF OTHER IMPERFECTIONS USUAL TO BEGINNERS IN RESPECT OF THE THIRD VICE, WHICH IS SPIRITUAL VOLUPTUOUSNESS

Other imperfections there are, besides those I here set forth under each vice, which beset many of these beginners, whereon, to avoid being prolix, I do not touch, limiting myself to some of the most conspicuous, which are, as it were, the origin and the cause of the rest. And in respect of the sin of lasciviousness, setting aside what it is to fall into this sin (since my intent is to deal with the imperfections which must be purged by the dark night), certain of these beginners contract imperfections which might be called spiritual lewdness; not because it is so, but that, when the soul receives spiritual delights, the body at times feels and experiences the same, by reason of its weakness. For it often happens that, even in the midst of spiritual exercises, and at times even when the spirit is deep in prayer or engaged in the Sacraments of Penance and the Eucharist, spontaneous notions and impulses of an unclean nature, impossible to check, are stirred up and impress themselves on the sensual part. The which, as I say, it being impossible to prevent, proceeds from one of three things.

The first sometimes proceeds (although not often, and only in weak constitutions), from the delight the body hath in spiritual things. For as the spirit and senses feel this delight, so doth each part of the physical man leap up to share in the same gratification, as far as its capacity and particular quality allow of. For then the spirit, which is the higher part, is moved to the refreshment and relish of God; and the sense, which makes up the inferior part, is moved to sensible relish and delight, as it cannot take nor feel any other. And thus it happens that the soul is in prayer with God as to the spirit; and on the other hand, in so far as it concerns the sense, she, not without her own deep disgust, passively experiences sensual rebellions and motions. For as, in short, these two parts form one whole, both, as a rule, share in what either of them receives, each after its fashion; for, as says the philosopher, whatever thing is received, is received according to the nature of the recipient. And so in these preliminary stages, and even when the soul is in a more advanced state, as the sensual part is imperfect, it takes advantage of the opportunity furnished to it by the spiritual delights of the soul to indulge its own peculiar delights with the imperfection that belongs to it. But when this sensitive part is, at length, reformed by the purgation of the dark night we are still to speak of, the soul ceases to have these weaknesses; for, so abundantly doth she receive the Divine Spirit, that rather doth it seem that it is she herself that is received into this Spirit; in short, as into the greater, and so preponderantly great. And so she experiences all these things after the fashion of the spirit, wherein she shares, united with God, in a marvelous way.

The second cause whence, at times, these rebellions proceed, is the devil, who, to disquieten and perturb the soul at such season as she is in prayer or desirous of obtaining it, does his best to provoke these unclean movements in the body: so that, if the soul takes any notice thereof, it causes her grave hurt. For, not only through dread thereof, so that she may set to work to struggle against them, does the soul relax in prayer, which is what he is after, but some even abandon it for good, since it seems to them that, in this exercise, they are more exposed to such things than out of it, as is the truth; for the devil tempts them more in this respect than any other, for the express purpose of making them abandon spiritual exercises. Nor is this all, but he succeeds in conjuring up before them, to the life, most hideous and loathsome objects, and at times in the closest connection with such spiritual things and people as do their souls most good, in order to terrify and bring them to utter destruction; so that they who take notice thereof dare not even to gaze or fix their attention on anything, lest immediately they stumble up against this or the other obstruction; particularly doth this apply to those of a melancholy turn of mind who are thereby so profoundly and violently affected that they are deeply to be pitied. But if melancholy itself be the cause and is at the bottom of these things, such people, as a rule, do not get rid of them until they recover from this quality of humor, unless, indeed, the dark night enters into the soul, which will gradually purify her entirely.

The third cause whence these lascivious motions are wont to proceed and wage war is usually the terror such people have conceived of these impure movements and images; for the horror of the sudden memory thereof flashing across their sight, or discourse, or thoughts, causes them to suffer these motions without any fault of their own.

Sometimes these spiritual people, when speaking of, or performing, spiritual devotions, are seized with a certain sort of exaltation and wildness of spirits caused by some reminiscence of the people nearest to them, whose intimacy they affect with a certain sort of frivolous relish; the which likewise springs from spiritual concupiscence (as we use the expression here), and sometimes excites in the will a pleasurable sensation.

Some acquire a liking to certain people in a spiritual way, which often springs from lust and not from spirit, the which is evident when, with the memory of this affection, the memory and love of God, instead of increasing, produces only remorse of conscience. For when love is purely spiritual, as it waxes stronger, so also doth that of God, and the more we dwell on it in our memory, so much the more do we cherish that of God and the more it makes us long for Him; the growth of the one keeping pace with the growth of the other. For the spirit of God hath this quality, that good increaseth good, inasmuch as there is likeness and conformity betwixt them. But when such love is born of sensual appetite, it works contrary effects; for the stronger the one grows so doth the other grow less, and the memory at the same time; for if this love increases, it will be instantly seen that we are waxing cold in that of God, and forgetting Him for the sake of this memory, although not without some remorse of conscience. And conversely, if the love of God increases in the soul, she waxes colder towards the other and forgets it; for as these loves are contrary one to the other, not only does the one not help the other, but, rather the predominant affection quenches and destroys it, and gathers fresh strength, as say the philosophers. Wherefore our Savior said in the Gospel: *Quod natum est ex carne, caro est: et quod natum est ex spiritu, spiritus est.*[3] What is born of flesh is flesh, and what is born of spirit is spirit; that is, the love that is born of sensuality, ends in sensuality, and that which is born of spirit, ends in the spirit of God, and He increases it a thousand fold. And this is the difference between these two loves, whereby they may be recognized. When the soul enters into the dark night, she puts all these variant loves in order. For she strengthens and purifies the one which is Godly; and the other she abandons or exterminates or mortifies, and, at first, she loses sight of both as will soon be told.

OF THE IMPERFECTIONS WHEREIN BEGINNERS FALL IN RESPECT OF THE SIN OF ANGER

By reason of the concupiscence which many beginners entertain for spiritual delights, their possession thereof is most often accompanied by many imperfections of the sin of anger. For, when the savor and relish in spiritual things is at an end, they naturally find themselves without force and spirit, and this uneasiness makes them bring their ill humor into their ordinary occupations, and wax angry at trifles, and at times, even, they become insufferable. The which often occurs after they have experienced a most delightful and sensible abstraction in prayer, for, when this gust and relish are over, naturally the body is left peevish and dull. Like to the child, when he is taken away from the breast he was enjoying to his heart's desire. In the which physical satiety, if they do not give way thereto there is nothing to blame, only an imperfection which must be purged in the aridness and conflict of the obscure night.

Of this sort, there are also other spiritually minded people who fall into a different kind of spiritual anger, which is, to wax wrath against the sins of others with a certain restless zeal, criticizing them, and at times impelled to scold them sourly, and this, in such a way, as if they had made themselves proprietors of virtue. All which is contrary to spiritual meekness.

There are others who, when they perceive their own imperfections, get angry against themselves; and that, not with humility but with such impatience, as they were fain to become saints in a day. Of these there are many who propose much, and make mighty resolutions, and, as they are not humble and are overconfident of themselves, the more resolutions they make, the deeper they fall and the angrier they get, being too impatient to wait until God shall give them sanctity at His own good pleasure; which is also contrary to the aforesaid spiritual meekness, and cannot be radically cured save by the purgation of the dark night; although some shew so much patience and proceed so slowly in this matter of wishing to improve, that God were fain to see less in them.

OF IMPERFECTIONS IN RESPECT OF SPIRITUAL GLUTTONY

As to the fourth vice, which is spiritual gluttony, there is much to say; for there is scarce one of these beginners who, however well he may proceed, falls not into somewhat of the many imperfections this vice gives rise to, by reason of the relish he finds, at first, in spiritual exercises. For many of these, spoilt by the flavor and relish they find in such exercises, try rather to give pleasure to the spiritual palate than to acquire true purity and devotion, which is what God looks at and accepts during the entire spiritual journey. Wherefore, over and above the imperfection that urges them to solicit these savors, the dainty they have already tasted makes them attempt to use the foot instead of the hand (begin where they should end), transgressing the limits of that middle course wherein virtue consists and is achieved. For, allured by the relish they find therein, some kill themselves with penances, and others weaken themselves with fasts, doing more than their bodily frailty suffers, without being ordered or advised thereto, nay, rather do they seek to evade him whom, in this matter they are bound to obey; and some even make bold to act in the manner thus described, although he has bidden them just the opposite. These are most imperfect, wrongheaded people, who set no store by subjection and obedience (which is a penance of the reason and freedom of choice), and therefore a more acceptable and savory sacrifice in the sight of God, than all others of corporal penance, which, apart from all else, is most imperfect because they are moved thereto solely by reason of the satisfaction and relish they find therein. Wherein, since all extremes are vicious, and by pursuing such a course, they follow their own will only, rather do they grow in vices than in virtues; for, to say the least of it, they become spiritual gluttons and wax in pride, because they walk not in obedience. And to such an extent doth the devil deceive many of these, adding fuel to the fire of their gluttony by gusts and appetites which he makes greater, that at length if they can do nought else, they change, or add to, or vary what is ordered them, because to them all obedience is gall and wormwood. Wherein some reach such a pitch of evil, that the mere fact that they go to these exercises at the precept of obedience deprives them of the desire and devotion to perform them, since their sole aim and delight is to do that the devil moves them to; all of which, perchance, were better left undone.

You shall see many of these extremely opinionated and contumacious with their spiritual master, in order to force him to assent to their likings, and they wrest his consent from him half by force, and if not, they bemoan themselves like children and sulk, and will do nothing heartily, and think they do not serve God when they are not allowed to follow their own bent. For as they have no mainstay save their own goodwill and pleasure, the moment it is taken from them, and it is sought to inspire them with the Will of God, they grow sad, and lose courage, and falter. These think that to please and satisfy themselves, is to serve and satisfy God.

There are others, also, who because of this dainty that has been vouchsafed them, so little realize their own wretchedness and baseness, and have so far flung aside the loving fear and respect they owe to God's greatness, that they hesitate not to argue vehemently with their confessors, as to whether they are to be permitted to confess and communicate frequently. And the worst of the matter is, that, often guided solely by their own opinion, they venture to communicate without the licence and approval of the minister and dispenser of Christ, and then try to hide from him the truth. And for this reason, with an eye to continue communicating, they make their confessions in any sort of slipshod fashion, being more eager to eat than to eat cleanly and worthily. As if it were not more healthy and holy, their inclinations tending otherwise, to beseech their confessors not to order them to approach the Sacred Feast so often; although of these two extremes, humble submission is better than either. But excessive daring paves the way for great evil, and they have reason to fear the chastisement that overtakes such boldness. When people of this sort communicate, all they hanker after is, to preserve some sensible relish or sensation rather than to reverence and worship God with heartfelt humility.

And in such sort do they annex this to themselves as a right, that when they have not derived some delight or sensible emotion, they think they have done nothing, judging most basely of God, and not perceiving that the least of the benefits this Most Holy Sacrament confers is that which touches the senses, and that incomparably the greatest is the invisible gift of Grace; since, in order to make them fix on Him the eyes of Faith, God often takes away these sensible pleasures and failures. And thus they are fain to feel God and taste of Him as if He were comprehensible and accessible, not only in this but in all other spiritual exercises. All of which is an exceeding great imperfection, and absolutely contrary to the condition of God, who demands the most absolute Faith.

In the prayer they practice these people do exactly the same, for they think the whole gist thereof consists in finding sensible delight and devotion, and they try to get it, as they say, by main force, and fatigue and weary the faculties and the brain. And when they have not found the said delight, they despond, thinking they have done nothing, and with this pretension of theirs they lose true devotion and spirit, which consists in persevering therein with patience and humility, distrustful of themselves, for the sake only of pleasing God. For this cause, when they have not found pleasure, if it be only for once, in this or the other exercise, they experience great distaste and repugnance to return thereto. For, in themselves they are, as we have said, like unto children, whose movements and actions are not ruled by reason but by inclination. They let all things else slide, whilst they seek after spiritual delight and comfort, and to this end, they are never done with reading books, and now they take up one meditation and now another, for all the world as if they went a chasing of their own pleasure in the things of God. The which God most justly, wisely, and lovingly denies, for, were it otherwise, they would, through this gluttony and spiritual fastidiousness, develop grave evils. Wherefore it behoves these greatly to enter into the dark night, so that they may be purged from these follies.

Those who are thus inclined to these pleasures are subject to another very grave imperfection, and it is that they are most weak and remiss in setting forth upon the rugged road of the Cross. For the soul which abandons herself to pleasing sensations, naturally finds all distastefulness of self-denial offensive. These are liable to many other imperfections, which all spring from this root, which the Lord cures in His own good season, by temptations, drynesses, and trials, for all these are part of the dark night. Whereon, not to wax lengthy, I will not dwell, save to say that spiritual sobriety and temperance bears another very different temper of mortification, fear, and submission in all her ways; admonishing us that the perfection and the value of things consists not in the number thereof, but in our own ability to deny ourselves therein; which they must strive their utmost to do, until God shall will to purify them in very truth, by making them enter into the dark night. In order to arrive thereat, I hasten forward in the declaration of these imperfections.

OF IMPERFECTIONS IN RESPECT OF ENVY AND SPIRITUAL SLUGGISHNESS

In respect, also, of the other two vices, which are envy and spiritual slothfulness, these beginners are not free from many imperfections. For as to envy, many of them are wont to suffer movements of vexation at the spiritual welfare of others; giving way to somewhat of sensible pain that they have been outstripped on the road, and they were fain not see them praised; for they wax sad at others' virtues, and at times, it becomes so unbearable to them that they deny them, undoing these praises as best they can, for they were fain to be preferred in all things. The which is most contrary to charity, which as St. Paul says rejoices in the truth.[4] And if charity can be envious at all, it is with a holy envy, grieved that it possesses not its neighbor's virtues, rejoicing in that he possesses them, and delighting in being outstripped by all the world beside in serving God, seeing that he, himself, falls so far short thereof.

In respect, also, of spiritual sloth, they are wont to find the most spiritual things tedious, and fly therefrom, as being such as clash most with sensible relish. For as they have been so pampered in spiritual things, the moment they find no favor therein, they become weary thereof. For, if only once, they find not in prayer that satisfaction their appetite craves (for, in short, it is meet that God deprives them thereof so as to prove them), they were fain to have nothing more to do therewith; at other times they forsake it entirely or go reluctantly. And so, by reason of their sluggishness, they postpone the journey of perfection (which is that of the denial of their own Will and pleasure for the sake of God), to the satisfaction and savor of the Will, which they go about to please after their own fashion more than that of God. And many of these were fain God's will coincided with their own, and become sad at having to bend their will to God's, and feel repugnance at being obliged to suit their will to the Divine. Whence, arises in them that they often think that what they find not to be their own will and pleasure, is not the Will of God; and, on the contrary, when they are satisfied, measuring God with themselves, and not themselves with God: a course quite opposite to what He Himself taught in the Gospel saying: *Qui autem periderit animam suam propter me, inveniet eam.*[5] That he that shall lose his will for Him, shall gain it; and he who shall gain his own will, shall lose it.

These, also, are full of disgust and weariness when they are bidden to do that for which they have no relish. And inasmuch as they follow after the gratification and savor of the spirit, like those brought up in luxury, they fly with gloom from everything harsh, being too weak to bear the strenuous discipline and labor of perfection, and take offense at the Cross, wherein are ciphered the delights of the spirit; and the more spiritual these things are, the greater weariness they feel. For, as they claim to proceed in spiritual things with full liberty, and as their will dictates, it fills them with invincible sadness and repugnance to enter upon the narrow road, which Christ calls that of Life.

Let it now suffice that we have singled out these imperfections, from amongst the many which habitually beset beginners, in this first stage, so that we may proceed to point out the need they are in, that God should set them into a state of greater advancement; the which is accomplished by His placing them in the dark night we shall now speak of; where, being weaned by God from the breasts of these relishes and suavities, in the midst of nought but aridnesses and inner darkness, He delivers them, by very different methods, from all these imperfections and follies and enables them to achieve virtue. For, however much the beginner may practice himself in mortifying in himself, all these, his actions and passions, he can never do so entirely, nor indeed ever so slightly, until God effects it in him by way of the purgation of the dark night. Whereof, so that I may say somewhat that may be useful, may God be pleased to give me His Divine Light, since it is indeed needed in so dark a night and difficult a matter.

WHEREIN IS EXPOUNDED THE FIRST LINE OF THE FIRST SONG, AND THE
EXPLANATION COMMENCED OF THIS DARK NIGHT

INTO THE DARKNESS OF THE NIGHT

This night, whereby we mean contemplation, produces in the spiritually minded two sorts of darkness or purgations, answering to the two parts of man, that is to say, the sensitive and spiritual. And thus, the first night or sensitive purgation is that wherein the soul purges and strips herself naked of all things of sense, by conforming the senses to the spirit; and the next is, the spiritual night or purgation, wherein the soul purges and denudes herself of all mental activity, by conforming and disposing the intellect for the union of love with God. The sensitive is usual and happens to many, and it is of these beginners, that we shall treat first. The spiritual purgation is gone through by very few, and those only who have been proved and tried, and of these we shall treat afterwards.

The first night or purgation is bitter and terrible to the sense. The second transcends all description, because it is exceeding fearsome for the spirit, as we shall presently shew: and as the sensitive comes first in order and takes place first, we shall briefly say somewhat thereof; so that we may proceed more especially to treat of the spiritual night, whereof very little has been said, either by word of mouth or writing, and moreover, because the experience thereof is extremely rare. Now, since the method these beginners pursue on the journey towards God is slavish and bears a strong resemblance to their own desires and delights, as was above set forth; since God wills to lead them higher, and deliver them from this base fashion of love to a loftier degree of love of God, and free them from the inadequate and mechanical exercise of the sense (the imagination) and mental activity which go agroping after God in such a feeble sort and with so much difficulty, as we have said, and places them in the exercise of the spirit, wherein they can communicate with God more abundantly and freer from imperfections; when, at length, they have practiced themselves for some time in the journey of virtue, persevering in meditation and prayer, wherein, with the suavity and relish they have found, they have become detached from worldly things, and acquired some spiritual strength in God, so as to be able to curb the creature appetites and in some small degree suffer for God some slight load and dryness, without turning back at the crucial moment; when, to their thinking, they are proceeding in these spiritual exercises to their entire satisfaction and delight; and when the Sun of Divine favors seems to them to shine most radiantly upon them, God darkens all this light, and shuts the door and fountain of the sweet spiritual water, which they were wont to drink in God as often and as long as they chose (since on account of their weakness and frailty, no door was shut to them), as saith Saint John in the Apocalypse: *Ecce dedi coram te ostium apertum, quod nemo potest claudere: quia modicam habes virtutem, et servasti verbum meum, et non negasti nomen meum,*[6] and thus, he leaves them in darkness so profound that they know not whither to direct the sense of the imagination and speculations of the mind. For they cannot take a single step towards meditation, as before they were wont, the interior sense being now submerged in this night, and made so barren, that not only find they no substance and delight in the spiritual matters and good practices wherein they were wont to rejoice and find relish, but, on the contrary, in its place a nauseous savor and bitterness. For, as I have said, as God knows them to have, at length, increased somewhat in growth; in order that they may acquire strength and escape from their swaddling clothes, He severs them His sweet breast, and putting them from His arms, teaches them to walk alone, the which, to them, is passing strange, as everything seems topsy-turvy.

This, in the case of people secluded from the world, usually takes place sooner after they have begun, than in that of others, inasmuch as they are freer from opportunities to turn back and more speedily reform their appetites for worldly things, which is what is absolutely necessary to enter into this happy night of sense. And, as a rule, it is not long after they begin, before they enter into this night of sense, and the greater number of them enter therein, for, usually, shall you see them fall into these drynesses.

Of this kind of sensitive purgation, inasmuch as it is so often met with, we might here quote large store of authorities from the Divine Scripture, where, at every step, we find many instances, particularly in the Psalms and Prophets; but, to avoid prolixity, we refrain therefrom, although we shall quote several later on.

OF THE SIGNS WHEREIN IT MAY BE PERCEIVED THAT THE SPIRITUALLY MINDED PERSON HAS COMMENCED HIS JOURNEY THROUGH THIS NIGHT AND SENSITIVE PURGATION

But as these drynesses may often arise, not from the said night and purgation of the sensitive appetite, but from sins or imperfections, remissness or lukewarmness, or from some ill-humor or indisposition of the body; I shall here set down a few signs whereby it may be known whether the dryness, in question, arises from the said purgation, or springs from any of the aforesaid vices; for which object, I find there are three principal signs.

The first is, if as he finds no suavity nor comfort in the things of God, so he finds none either in any other created thing. For, as God places the soul in the obscure night so as to dry and purge her of the sensitive appetite, he lets her find pleasure or savor in nothing. Wherein is credibly seen that this dryness and inappetency does not proceed from sin nor from imperfections freshly committed. For, if this were so, she would, perforce, feel in the natural disposition, some tendency or desire to take joy in something other than the things of God. For, whenever the appetite lapses into some imperfection, it soon feels itself drawn towards it, much or little, in the like degree as was the desire and affection it bestowed thereon. But as this want of relish in things above and below, may proceed from some physical indisposition or melancholy humor, the which doth often not allow them to take pleasure in anything, the second sign and condition is essential.

The second sign and condition of this purgation is, that, as a rule, the memory is constantly fixed on God, with anxiety and painful watchfulness, since, when she sees herself without her former relish for the things of God, the soul thinks that she doth not serve God, but is going backwards. And herein is seen that this want of appetite and dryness does not arise from coldness and lukewarmness; since it is of the very nature of lukewarmness not to care nor to feel interior solicitude for the things of God. Wherefore betwixt dryness and lukewarmness there is a great difference. Because lukewarmness is subject to great remissness and slackening of the will and courage, and all solicitude to serve God is absent: whereas merely purgative dryness carries with it a constant anxiety accompanied by regret and pain, that the soul, as I say, doth not serve God. And this, although sometimes increased by melancholy or other humor (as at other times it is) fails not to work its purgative effect on the appetite; since the soul is entirely bereft of relish and sets her attention solely upon God; because, when it arises from sheer bodily indisposition, everything becomes distasteful and a source of uneasiness to the physical constitution, which feels no longer those desires to serve God which belong to the purgative dryness, whereby, although the sensitive part is greatly depressed, and too weak and frail to act, by reason of the little relish it finds, the spirit, nevertheless, is alert and strong.

The cause of this dryness is, because God transfers the properties and strength of the sense to the spirit; and the sense and natural strength of the sensitive part, by reason of their incapacity, being deprived thereof, they remain hungry, parched and empty. For the sensitive part has no skill in that which is pure spirit; and so, when the spirit finds sweet relish, the flesh is vexed and loses its energies to act: but the spirit, which is then engaged in receiving the Divine food, proceeds stoutly, and more alertly and solicitously than before in her watchfulness not to fail towards God; although, it does not at once experience spiritual savor and delight, but dryness and displeasure, by reason of the novelty of the change. For, as the spiritual palate has become accustomed to those former sensible gusts, it still keeps its eyes thereon. And, also, because the spiritual palate has not been made fit and purged for so subtle a pleasure, and cannot taste the spiritual delight and goodness, only aridness and distaste, for lack of that it formerly with such ease enjoyed, until it has been gradually disposed thereto, step by step, by means of this dry and obscure night.

For those whom God begins to lead through these solitudes of the desert are like to the sons of Israel, who directly God began to give them in the desert food from Heaven so delicate, that as the text says, it was converted into the flavor of each one's favorite food; withal, they felt more keenly the loss of the gusts and relishes of the flesh meat and onions they eat before in Egypt, whereto their palate was accustomed and longed after, rather than the delicate sweetness of the angelic sustenance, and they wept and groaned for meat amidst the food from Heaven: *Recordamur piscium, quos comedabamus in Egypto gratis: in mentem nobis veniunt cucumeres et pepones porrique, et cepe, et allia.*[7] For, to such a depth doth the baseness of our appetite reach, that it makes us long after our miserable trifles, and loathe the incommutable treasure of Heaven. But, as I say, when these aridnesses arise from the purgative stage of the sensible appetite, although, at first, the spirit finds no relish, by reason of the causes we have just mentioned, it is inspired with strength and courage to act, by the nourishment it receives from the interior food, the which food is the preliminary of dry and obscure contemplation for the sense; the which contemplation is, as a rule, hidden and secret from him who himself possesses it; together with this aridness and emptiness it effects in the senses, it inclines and fills the soul with longing for solitude and silence, without the power to think on any particular thing, or wish to think. And if those, to whom this happens, were able, at this time, to keep perfectly still and refrain from all interior and exterior action, and make no attempt to procure such by their own efforts and mental activity, but, free from all anxiety, abandon themselves entirely to the guidance of God, waiting for His coming and listening for His voice with an interior and loving attention; they would, soon, in this abstraction and vacancy of mind, feel this interior refreshment bestowed most delicately upon them. The which is so delicate, that, as a rule, if they are over-desirous or solicitous to feel it, they feel it not; for, as I say, it operates in the most intense suspension or abstraction of the soul; since it is like the air, which, if one tries to imprison in one's fist, is gone. And this is what we may take to be the meaning of the words spoken by the Spouse to His Belovèd in the Canticles, to wit: *Averte oculos tuos à me, quia ipsi me avolare fecerunt.*[8] Turn away thine eyes from me, for they overcome me. For, after such a fashion doth God place the soul in this state and by so different a road doth He lead her, that if she is fain to take action of herself and make use of her own powers, rather doth she hinder than assist the operation that God is working in her; the which, before was quite the reverse. The cause is, that, whereas, in this state of contemplation, which is when the soul goes forth from all mental activity and speculation of her own, to the state of the progressives, it is God who now works upon her; in such a way that, it seems as if He bound up the interior powers, leaving her no support in the mind, nor substance in the will, nor motion in the memory. For, at this season, whatever the soul may accomplish of herself, serves for no other purpose save, as we have said, to interrupt and hinder the interior peace, and the operation which, in this barrenness of the sense, God works in the spirit. The which, forasmuch as it is spiritual and delicate, the effects it produces are quiet and delicate, peaceful and very far away from those other former delights, which were exceeding palpable and sensible. For this peace is that spoken of by David, breathed into the soul of God to render her spiritual: *Quonian loquetur pacem in plebem suam.*[9] And hence we come to the third sign.

The third sign whereby we may perceive this to be the purgation of the sense, is that the soul can no longer, for all her striving, meditate nor send her thoughts abroad, by means of the sense of the imagination, so as to stimulate her motions, as she was wont; because, as in this case, God begins to communicate Himself to her no longer through the senses as He did before, by means of the mental combination and analysis of their own ideas by the reasoning and discursive faculties, but in pure spirit, wherein there is no consecutive exercise of intellectual thought, and as He communicates Himself to her in an act of absolute contemplation, whereto the exterior or interior senses of the lower part cannot reach: hence it is that the imagination and fancy can furnish no support, nor set the springs thereof in motion by meditation, nor yet find any footing therein, from that time forth.

By this third sign, it may be known that this hindrance of the faculties and the slight disgust they experience, doth not arise from any evil humor (bodily indisposition); for when such is the case, as soon as the humor, which is never permanent, is dissipated, then, the soul if she is bent thereon however slightly, is again able to perform what she did before, and the faculties find their customary supports. The which is not so in the purgation of the appetite; for, when one begins to enter therein, the inability to make use of the faculties in thought and speculation increases. For, although it is true that this condition, with some, is not, at first, of such persistent duration as to prevent them from being carried away by sensible comforts and delights (since on account of their weakness it was not advisable to wean them abruptly), nevertheless it continues to increase and gradually make an end of the sensitive operations, that is, if they are to advance still further; for, those who do not take the way of contemplation, entertain a very different method; in whom this night of barrenness is not wont to be continuous for the senses; since although they sometimes experience it, at others they do not; and although sometimes they are deprived of the use of intellectual thought, yet, at others, they are able to avail themselves thereof, solely because God places them in this night to teach them by practice, humble them, and reform the appetite, so that they may not be bred up on dainties; and not in order to lead them to the spiritual road which is this contemplation. For God doth not lead all who, of set purpose, practice themselves in this journey of the spirit, to perfect contemplation: wherefore He alone knoweth. Hence it is, that these never succeed in severing the senses from the breasts they cling to, of meditation and mental activity, save for some brief moments and intermittently, as we have said.

AS TO HOW WE SHOULD DEMEAN OURSELVES IN THIS DARK NIGHT

In the season, then, of the drynesses of this sensitive night (wherein God effects the change we have above spoken of), leading forth the soul from the way of the sense to that of spirit, that is from meditation to contemplation (wherein the soul of herself and her own powers can neither perform nor think on things of God, as has been said), spiritual people undergo great affliction; not so much for the aridness they suffer, as for the dread that besets them that they have gone astray along this road, thinking that spiritual goodness has deserted them and that God has forsaken them, since they find no support nor delight in any good thing. Then they fatigue themselves and try (as they were wont) to bend the faculties (not without some relish) to some object of mental thought, thinking that when they do not achieve this, and do not feel that they are occupied, they do nothing; the which they accomplish, not without great interior aversion and repugnance of the soul which rejoiced to be in this quiet and repose. Whereby dallying with the one, they make no progress in the other; because, for the sake of exercising the mind, they lose the spirit they had of tranquillity and peace, and thus they are like to one who leaves what he has finished, to commence it afresh; or to one who went forth from the city to go back into it again; or one who abandons the chase to follow it anew: and, in this stage, such action is superfluous, since they will find nothing, and merely revert to their first method of proceeding, as has been said.

At this season, if there is no one at hand to understand and direct them, such people as these turn back, either forsaking the road entirely or losing all energy, or, at least, they are hindered from advancing further, by the pains they are at to travel on the first road of meditation and mental activity, wearying and straining the physical powers most unnecessarily and imagining that they fail thereof by their own negligence or sins. The which is now superfluous; for, at last, God leads them by another road, which is that of contemplation (absorption), absolutely at variance with the first; for the one is that of meditation and mental exercise, and the other falls not within the scope of either imagination or intellect. They that shall see themselves in such a sort must take comfort, and persevere patiently, and, not giving way to grief, confide in God, who doth not forsake those who seek Him with an upright and simple heart, nor shall fail to give them all things necessary for the journey, until He leads them forth into the clear and pure light of love, which He will give them by means of the following dark night of the spirit, if it so be, that they deserve that He should place them therein.

The method they must abide by in this night of the senses, is to be utterly indifferent as to mental exercise and meditation: since now, as I have said, the time for this is past, but to leave the soul in peace and quiet, however much they may think they do nothing and are losing time and that their desire to think of nothing in this state comes of their own sluggishness. For, if they will only have patience and persevere in prayer, and leave the Soul free and unfettered, unruffled by any manner of impression or thought, free from all anxiety as to what they shall think upon and meditate, being satisfied with a loving and restful waiting upon God, devoid of all solicitude, activity, and excessive longing to feel and taste Him, they shall, indeed, accomplish a great matter. For all these strivings and efforts trouble and distract the soul from the peaceful quietude and sweet repose of contemplation bestowed in this state. And, whatever be the scruples that beset her that she is losing time and that it would be wise to occupy herself about something else, since in prayer, she can nor do nor think ought: let her resign herself and be at peace, just as if she resorted to prayer for no other end save her own solace and liberty of spirit. For if, of herself, she tries to stir up the interior powers, it would be to hinder and lose the graces which God, by means of this peace and repose of the soul, is fixing and imprinting on her. Just as a painter limning a face, if the face were to move about from side to side bent on some other occupation, the painter would be hindered in his work and able to produce nothing: so when the soul is in peace and inward repose, any movement and eagerness or painstaking attention on her part at such a time will distract and disquiet her, and is bound to produce in her a feeling of aridness and emptiness of sense. For the more she were fain to lean upon any support of emotion and impression, so much the more keenly will she feel its lack, the which cannot now be compensated for by such a method. Whence, in this state, this said soul should take no notice that she has been bereft of the operations of the faculties, rather rejoice that she loses them so soon. For, if she does not hinder the operation of the infused contemplation that God continues to give, so is she refreshed with the more undisturbed abundance and the opportunity bestowed upon her to burn and be kindled in the spirit of love, which this dark and hidden contemplation brings with it and instils into the soul.

I were fain, notwithstanding, that from this no general rule should be deduced, to abandon meditation or mental speculation; for the forsaking thereof should always arise from want of power to do otherwise, and that, for such time only as, by way of purgation and torment, or through most perfect contemplation, the Lord himself checks it. For at other times and seasons, this stay and refuge must always be resorted to, and more especially the consideration suggested by the life and Cross of Christ, which are best suited for purgation and patience and a safe and sure journey, and is an admirable guide to the heights of contemplation. The which is nothing else but a secret, tender, and loving infusion of God which, if we oppose no obstacle, inflames the soul in the spirit of love, as she herself sets forth in the following line.

WHEREIN ARE EXPOUNDED THE THREE LINES OF THE SONG

WITH HEARTACHE KINDLED INTO LOVE

This flaming up of love is not, as a rule, felt at first, as it has not yet begun to set fire to the heart, either on account of bodily[10] impurity, or because the soul, failing to understand its nature, doth not, as we have said, procure for it within herself a peaceable admittance, entry and refuge. But, at times, with or without this, a certain sense of longing for God begins to make itself felt; and the more it increases so doth the soul feel more and more enraptured by, and inflamed in, the love of God, without knowing or understanding how and whence springs up in her this said love and tenderness, save that this flame and kindling seems to her to grow at times so strong within her, that sick for very love, she pants after God; like as did David, who, when in this night, described his own sensations in these words: *Quid inflammatum est cor meum, et renes mei commutati sunt: et ego ad nihilum redactus sum, et nescivi.* Because my heart was ablaze (that is: in contemplative love), my tastes and affections were changed likewise; to wit, from the sensitive way to the spiritual, by this holy aridness and cessation wherein they are all plunged, that we proceed to describe. And I, says he, was melted and reduced to nothing, and I knew not. Because, as we have said, without knowing whither she goes, the soul sees herself reduced to nothing in respect of all things above or below wherein she was wont to delight; and solely perceives herself filled with love without knowing how. And since, at times, the blaze of love in the spirit waxes great, the longings of the soul after God are so strong that the very bones seem to be parched up with this thirst, and the body to sicken, and its vitality and strength to be consumed in the acuteness of this love, and the soul feels this thirst of love to be intense. The which David also experienced and felt when he says: *Sitivit anima mea ad Deum vivum.*[11] My soul thirsted for the living God; which is as much as to say: Sharp was the thirst that beset my soul. The which thirst in respect of its intensity, we may say, kills with thirst. Although the vehemence of this thirst is not continuous save at times, nevertheless some thirst is regularly experienced. And it must be noted here that, as I have begun to show, this love is not usually felt at first, only the dryness and emptiness we now describe; and that, in place of this love which afterwards comes to be kindled, the soul, in the midst of these aridnesses and emptiness of the powers, is constantly engrossed by an undivided attention to, and solicitude after God, whereto is added an abiding pain and dread that she serves Him not; for it is a sacrifice that pleases God not a little to see the spirit troubled and afflicted for His love's sake. This secret contemplation it is that imprints this anxiety in the soul until such time as it shall, in some measure, have purged the sense, that is, the sensitive part, from the natural strength and affections by means of these aridnesses wherein it places her, it proceeds to kindle in the spirit this love Divine. But until this takes place, in short like a sick man undergoing a cure, the soul experiences nought but suffering and a withering purgation of the appetite in this obscure night, wherein she is healed of many imperfections and proved in many virtues, to the end that she may be made capable of receiving the aforesaid love, as shall now be shown in the following line:

Oh gladsome hap!

Forasmuch as God sets the soul in this dark night to the end that, the sense of the inferior part be purged, and prepared for, subjected to, and joined with, the spirit, by casting it into darkness and making it to cease from mental activity; so also, afterwards, He places her in spiritual night to the end that she may be purified in order to be united with God, wherein she acquires (although she is far from thinking it), so many benefits, that she holds it for a gladsome hap to have escaped from the snares and limitations of the sense of the inferior part through this happy night, as the verse before us says, to wit, "Oh gladsome hap!" As to which we must here note the benefits that the soul finds in this night, by reason whereof, she holds it for a fortunate chance to pass therethrough: all which benefits are embraced in the following line:

I stole me forth unseen.

By the which stealing forth, is meant the escape of the soul from the bondage wherein she was held by the sensitive part, which interposed its own weak, cribbed, and dangerous processes (as those of this inferior part are) between her and her search for God; since, at every step they made her stumble up against a thousand imperfections and follies, as we have above pointed out under the seven capital vices. Wherefrom she is entirely delivered by all her gusts, (whether from above or below), being extinguished, and all her intellectual powers darkened in this night, which bestows on her other innumerable graces in the conquest of virtue, as we shall now shew; for it will be a most pleasant and comforting consideration for him who travels on this road, to see how a thing that seems so harsh and adverse to the soul, performs in her so many graces. All of which are won (as we say), by the soul going forth, as her affections and motions urge, into the midst of this night, from all created things, wherein she starts upon her journey to things eternal, which is, indeed, an exceeding happiness and good fortune. Firstly, on account of the immense mercy it is, to quench the appetite and affection in regard to all things. Secondly, because they who endure and persevere in entering by this narrow gate and strait and arduous road which leads to life, are exceeding few, as saith our Savior: *Quam angusta porta, et arcta via est, quæ ducit ad vitam: et pauci sunt, qui inveniunt eam.*[12] For the narrow door is this night of the sense, wherefrom, in order to enter thereat, the soul is stripped naked and denuded, being directed by Faith which is aloof from all sense, to take that other and narrower road whereon she must afterwards pursue her journey under the guidance of most absolute Faith, which is the link whereby she is united with God. Upon which road, forasmuch as it is so straight, dark, and terrible (so much so that there is no comparison between this night of the sense to that of the spirit in respect of its darkness and conflicts, as we shall shew), although there are exceeding few that travel it, yet their conquests are incomparably greater. Whereof we shall now commence to say somewhat with all possible brevity, so as to pass on to the following night.

OF THE BENEFITS PRODUCED IN THE SOUL BY THIS NIGHT OF SENSE

This night and purgation of the appetite, of such fair augury for the soul by reason of the marvelous graces and benefits it endues her with (although she herself thinks, as we have said, that it rather deprives her of them), for like as Abraham made high festival when his son Isaac was weaned, so is there rejoicing in Heaven when, at last, God unswathes the soul from out her swaddling clothes, and lowers her from His arms, making her to walk on her own feet; and weaning her from the milk and soft and honeyed food of children, gives her to eat of bread with crust, so that she may begin to relish the food of grown up men which, in these drynesses and darkness of the senses, He begins to give to the spirit empty and barren of the substance of the senses; which is the infused contemplation we have mentioned. And this is the first and principal conquest of the soul, whence all the rest derive.

Of these the first is the knowledge of ourselves and of our misery. Because apart from the fact that God generally bestows these benefits upon the soul, swathed about with this knowledge; these drynesses and emptiness of the faculties so different from the abundance she before enjoyed, and the difficulty she finds in devout matters, force upon her the knowledge of her own baseness and wretchedness which, in the season of her prosperity, she was blind to. Of this there is a fine image in Exodus, wherein, it being God's will to humble the sons of Israel and to force them to realize who and what they were, He bade them remove and strip off the gala robes and festival adornments wherewith they usually went about clothed in the desert, saying: *Jam nunc depone ornatum tuum.*[13] Now, from henceforth put off thy finery and festal robes, and clothe ye with common working garments, to the end that ye may know the treatment ye deserve. Which is as if He had said: Forasmuch as the dress you wear, being that of feasting and rejoicing, exposeth you not to perceive the enormity of your baseness, remove this raiment, so that, henceforth, seeing yourselves clad in vileness, you may know your own unworthiness and who you are. Whence, also, the soul comes to realize her own misery which before was hidden from her. Because, in the season she went about holiday making, as it were, and found in God great delight and comfort and support, she proceeded with somewhat more of contentment and satisfaction, being convinced that to a certain extent, her deeds were directed to His service. For, although these people may not own it to themselves expressly, yet there is an inkling of something of the sort in the satisfaction they find in the delights bestowed upon them. But, now, clad in this other sort of work-a-day garb of difficulty, dryness, and desolation, her former lanthorns dimmed, the soul possesses and acquires in downright earnest this so excellent and necessary a virtue of self-knowledge, and at last holds herself as nought and takes no sort of satisfaction in herself, because she sees that of herself she does, and can do, nothing. And this lack of satisfaction with herself and the affliction that overwhelms her in that she serves not God, God holds and esteems more highly than all the previous deeds and gustos she performed and experienced, however numerous they may have been. Forasmuch as they exposed her to many imperfections and follies; and from this vesture of aridness proceeds not only that we have said, but also the benefits we shall now proceed to state and many more which we shall leave unsaid, as from their origin and fount, from the knowledge of ourselves.

As to the first, the soul is impelled to converse with God with greater reverence and ceremony, which must never be absent from our intercourse with the Almighty. The which in the prosperous season of her delight and comfort, she overlooked; for, the very favor she enjoyed made her wax somewhat bolder and less reverential than behoved her. Like as happened to Moses when he heard God's voice who, carried away by his delight and longing, without further consideration, was emboldened to approach, had God not bidden him to stop and loose the shoes from off his feet: *Ne appropies, inquit, huc: solve calceamentum de pedibus tuis.*[14] Whereby is manifested the reverence and respectful bearing in nakedness of appetite, wherewith we must converse with God. Whence, when Moses complied with, he became so absolutely obedient and circumspect, that as the Scripture saith, not only dared he not draw nigh, but he did not even make so bold as look on God. Because, having removed the shoes of his appetites and pleasures, he profoundly realized his own misery before God: for, so it behoved him in order to hear the Divine words. Also the ability bestowed on Job by God to speak with Him, did not spring from those delights and blessedness that Job himself mentions, as being wont to pass between himself and God, but from his being set naked on a dung heap, forsaken and even persecuted by his friends, full of anguish and bitterness, and the ground alive with worms: and then, after such sort as this did the Almighty God, who raises the poor from filth, deign to hold communion with him with greater abundance and far more sweetness, revealing to him the lofty heights of His Wisdom, than He had never seen fit to do in the season of his prosperity.

And now, since we have chanced to touch thereon, we must point out another excellent benefit there is in this dark night and dryness of the sensitive appetite, and it is, that in this dark night, in order that the words of the prophet should be fulfilled: *Oriteur in tenebris lux tua*.[15] Thy light shall shine on the darkness; God enlightens the soul, not only by making her to know her own misery and baseness, as we have said, but, also, His own grandeur and excellence. Because, apart from the sensible appetites and gusts and supports being entirely annihilated, the intellect is left clear and limpid to perceive the truth; because all sensible gust and appetite, even although in spiritual things, clouds and impedes the mind, likewise, also, the constriction and dryness of the sense illuminates and gives life to the intellect, as says Isaiah: *Vexatio intellectum dabit auditui*.[16] That oppression shews how God proceeds to instruct the naked and enfranchised soul (the which is absolutely necessary in order to receive His divine influence) supernaturally and by means of this dark and obscure night of contemplation, in His Divine Wisdom: the which He did not do in the previous succulence and delights. This the prophet Isaiah admirably sets forth, saying: *Quem docebit scientiam? Et quem intelligere faciet auditum? Ablactos à lacte, avulsos ab uberibus.*[17] To whom shall God teach His knowledge, and whom shall He make to hear His word? To those weaned from the milk and to those severed from the breast.

Wherein is made manifest that the former milk of spiritual sweetness and the stay afforded by the breast of the savory disquisitions of the sensitive faculties which the soul was wont to relish, do not so much dispose her for this Divine influence as the lack of the first and the withdrawal of the other. Wherefore, in order to hearken to this great King with all due reverence, the Soul must stand exceeding firm and lean on no support of affection or sense, as Habakkuk says of himself: *Super custodiam meam stabo, et figam gradum super munitionem: et contemplabor, ut videam, quid dicatur mihi.*[18] I will stand over my tabernacle (that is not stayed up by appetite), and I will make fast my foot (that is, I will not lean on intellectual reasoning), so that I may contemplate and hear that which God shall say to me. So that we have now arrived at this result, that, from this night comes primarily knowledge of ourselves whence, as from a foundation, springs this other knowledge of God. Wherefore St. Augustine said to God: Let me know myself, O Lord, and I shall know Thee. For as philosophers say one extreme may be known by the other. And in order more fully to prove the efficacy this sensitive night possesses, in its aridness and desolation, to increase the light which the soul, as we were saying, now receives from God, we shall quote that text of David, wherein he clearly sets forth the great power this night bestows to reach this lofty knowledge of God. These, then, are his words: *In terra deserta, et invia, et inaquosa: sic in sancto apparui tibi, ut viderem virtutem tuam, et gloriam tuam.*[19] In the desert land, without water, parched and where no road was, I appeared before Thy face so as to be able to see Thy power and glory. The which is a wonderful thing (although David does not say so here), that it was not by the many spiritual delights and gusts he had received that he was disposed and fitted to know the Glory of God, but by aridness and severance from the sensitive part, which is here shadowed forth under the parched and desert land. Neither does he say that the speculations and Divine meditations, to which he so often betook himself, led him to feel and see the power of God, but his own inability to fix his thoughts on God, and the want of guidance he found in the disquisitions of imaginary considerations, whereby is meant the land without a road. So that, if we would indeed arrive at the Knowledge of God and of ourselves, the only way is by this dark night with its aridness and emptiness, although not with the same plentitude and abundance as in the following night of the spirit; because this knowledge is, as it were, the root of the next.

In the drynesses and emptiness of this night of the appetite the soul also acquires humility, which is the contrary virtue to the first capital vice which we stated to be spiritual pride. By this humility which she achieves through the said knowledge of herself, she purges herself from all those imperfections wherein she fell in the season of her prosperity. Because, perceiving her own barrenness and wretchedness, she is free from the faintest motion of any thought that she is better than others or that she has in anyway outstripped them, as she did before, rather, on the contrary, doth she recognize that they are in a better way than herself. And hence springs love towards her neighbor; because she respects and doth not judge, as before she did, when she perceived her own intense fervor and none in others; she realizes her own baseness only and keeps it ever before her eyes, to such an extent that it does not admit of, nor give room for, her to fix them on any other person. The which, David, being in this night, admirably expresses, saying: *Obmutui, et humiliatus sum, et silui à bonis: et dolor meus renovatus est.*[20] I was dumb and was humiliated and held my peace even from good, and my sorrow was renewed. This he says, because it seemed to him that the treasures of his soul were so utterly brought to nought, that not only was there no speech, nor could none be found thereof; but, in respect of those of others, he was likewise dumb with the grief of the knowledge of his misery.

In this state, also, those we are speaking of become submissive and obedient in this, their spiritual journey. For as they so keenly perceive their own wretchedness, not only do they listen to their teachers, but even desire to be directed and counselled by anyone , whosoever he may be. The presumptuousness that, at times, they entertained in their season of prosperity leaves them; and finally all the imperfections we have pointed out, under the head of spiritual pride, are swept away as they advance further on their journey.

OF OTHER BENEFITS THIS NIGHT OF SENSE PRODUCES IN THE SOUL

As to the imperfections these beginners were wont to entertain in regard to spiritual avarice in which they coveted this and the other spiritual gift, and the Soul was never satisfied with these and the other exercises, so great was her sensual cupidity and the relish she found therein, now in this dark and thirsty night, she walks reformed indeed. For, as she no longer finds the same delight and savor as before, rather nausea and difficulty, she makes use of them with such moderation that, perchance, she is now as much exposed to lose by remissness, as before she lost by excess; although to those whom God places in this night, he generally gives humility and promptness, but yet not without nausea, to the end that they perform what they are bidden for the sake of God alone; and they get quit of many things, because they find no relish therein.

As to spiritual voluptuousness, it is also clearly seen that by this same aridness and physical nausea which repels the soul in spiritual things, she shakes herself loose from these impurities we there pointed out; which, as we stated, generally proceeded from the fortuitous overflowing of the delight experienced by the spirit into the senses.

But as to the imperfections in respect of the fourth vice, which is spiritual gluttony, whereof the soul rids herself in this dark night, they may be seen under that heading, although inasmuch as they are innumerable they are not all set down; and, therefore, I shall not refer to them here, for I were now fain to bring this night to a close, so as to pass on to the next, wherein we shall find grave doctrine. Suffice it therefore to say, in order to gauge the numberless graces which, besides those mentioned, the soul achieves in this night against the vice of spiritual gluttony, that she delivers herself from all those imperfections there set down, and from many other and graver evils than are there mentioned, wherein many we have known have fallen, because they had not reformed their desire for this spiritual dainty. Because, as God in this dark and arid night wherein He places the soul, reins in the concupiscence, and curbs the appetite after such sort that it may scarce admit of any longing for anything whether of Heaven or earth; and gradually increases

this until, as the soul becomes reformed, mortified, and strengthened in order of her concupiscence and desires, her passions seem
to lose their strength; whereupon, by means of this spiritual sobriety, besides those already mentioned, marvelous gifts are conferred
upon her; because, with this mortification of her desires and concupiscence, she dwells in spiritual tranquillity and peace; for where
desire and concupiscence no longer reigns, disquiet cannot enter,
only God's peace and comfort.

Hence proceeds another second benefit, and it is, that the soul
bears about with her a constant memory of God, with a dread and
error of falling back, as we have said, on the spiritual road; the which
is a great mercy, and not of the least, in this dryness and purgation of
the appetite, because the soul is purified and cleansed from the imperfections which clung to her by reason of her appetites and affections,
which of themselves, blunt and obscure her radiance. There is
another very great benefit for the soul in this night and it is, that she
applies herself to virtue wholesale, as it were, such as patience and
long suffering which she indeed learns by practice in these drynesses
and emptiness, and patience to persevere in spiritual exercises without
comfort and without relish. She is practiced in the charity of God,
since she is no longer moved by the taste and savor she finds in
the matter, but by God alone. Likewise she now practices the virtue of
fortitude, because in these difficulties and nauseas she finds in action,
she draws strength from weakness, and so waxes strong; and, finally,
in these drynesses, the soul is exercised in all virtues, whether cardinal,
theological, or moral. And that, in this night, the soul achieves all
these four benefits we have here set down, to wit: the great delight of
peace, a constant memory of God, and her own cleanness and purity,
besides the practice of the virtues we have just named, is declared by
David like as he had himself made trial thereof, when he was plunged
into this night, in these words: *Renuit consolari anima mea, memor fui
Dei, et delectatus sum, et exercitatus sum, et defecit spiritus meus.*[21] My soul
rejected consolation, I remembered God, I found comfort and exercised
myself, and my spirit died within me. And immediately thereupon,
he says: I meditated in my heart by night, and exercised myself, and
swept and purified my spirit[22]: to wit, of all affections.

In respect of the imperfections of the other three spiritual vices we there spoke of, which are envy, wrath, and slothfulness, the soul is also purged in this drought of the appetite and acquires the opposite virtues thereto. For, softened and humiliated by these aridnesses and difficulties and other temptations and trials wherein God proves her in many other ways than by this night, she becomes gentle in regard to God and in regard to herself, and also as regards her neighbor. So that she no longer waxes passionately wrathful against herself for her own faults, nor against her neighbors for theirs, nor does she harbor insolent discontent and displeasure against God, because He does not make her righteous all at once. Then, as to envy, she now also bears charity towards others; for, if she feels any envy, it is no longer vicious as before, when it was grievous to her that others should be preferred before her and bear away the palm: for to her now, at length, it has been given in the perception of her own utter misery; and the envy she feels (if any there is) is virtuous, desiring to imitate them, the which is great virtue.

Neither is the sluggishness and tediousness she now feels in spiritual things vicious as of yore; for that she entertained proceeded from the spiritual relishes which, at times, she experienced, and tried to procure when they were absent. But this weariness does not proceed from any failure to obtain spiritual delight; because God has rid them of it in all things in this purgation of the appetite.

Besides these benefits we have said, the soul secures innumerable others by means of this arid contemplation. Because, in the midst of these aridnesses and conflicts, often when she least expects it, God communicates to her a spiritual suavity and most pure love, and spiritual impressions at times surpassingly exquisite, each one of which is infinitely more valuable and costly than anything she tasted of before. Although the soul cannot be brought to think so, at first; for the spiritual influence she now receives is most delicate and imperceptible to the sense.

Finally, inasmuch as the soul is now purged of her affections and sensitive[23] desires, she achieves liberty of spirit, wherein she gradually conquers the twelve fruits of the Holy Ghost. Now, also, she is marvelously delivered from the grasp of her three enemies, the World, the Flesh, and the devil; for with the extinction of the savor and sensitive relish respecting all things, nor devil, nor World, nor sensuality have arms or strength against the spirit.

These drynesses, then, make the soul to walk with purity in the love of God; since she is no longer moved to action by the relish and savor as was, perchance, the case when she experienced delight; save solely to please God. She ceases to be presumptuous and self-complacent, as, perchance, she was wont to be in the season of her prosperity, but fearful and uncertain of herself, not being satisfied with herself in anything: wherein consists the only fear which conserves and increases virtue. This dryness, likewise, quenches her concupiscences and the high carriage of her temper, as has been said. For now, were it not for the relish that God of His good pleasure vouchsafes sometimes to infuse in her, it is rarely that she finds sensible delight and comfort by her own industry and efforts in any spiritual work and exercise, as has already been said above.

In this dark and arid night, this blessed soul grows in the fear of God, and anxiety to serve Him. For, as the breasts of sensuality, wherewith she fed and cherished the appetites whose lures she followed, are gradually withered up, her longing to serve God alone remains fixed, stubborn and naked, which is a thing most pleasing in His sight. For as says David: *Sacrificium Deo spiritus contribulatus.*[24] The afflicted spirit is a sacrifice to God. As the soul, therefore, knows that in this arid purgation where through she has passed, she has derived and acquired such precious gifts, and their number so great as has been here related, she does not exaggerate when she gives voice to this line of the song we are explaining,

> Oh gladsome hap!
> I sallied forth by none perceived.

That is, I escaped from the bonds and slavery of the sensitive appetites and affections, without being seen; to wit, the three aforesaid enemies were powerless to bar my way. The which (as we have said), bind and hold back the soul through her appetites and pleasures, without which they cannot wage war against her, as has been said, so that she may not go forth from herself into the liberty of the perfect love of God.

Whence, the four passions of the soul, which are joy, grief, hope and fear, being silenced by constant mortification; and the natural appetites in the sensual part being lulled to sleep by constant aridness; and the harmony of the senses and interior powers ceasing from their discursive motions and mental operations, as we have said, the which constitutes the whole population and dwelling place of the inferior part of the soul: they cannot hinder this spiritual freedom, and the house is left in silence and at peace, as says the following verse.

WHEREIN IS EXPOUNDED THE LAST LINE OF THE FIRST SONG

MY HOUSE BEING NOW AT PEACE

This house of our sensuality being now at rest, that is, its passions mortified, its greedinesses extinguished, and the appetites asleep and deadened by means of this happy night of sensitive purgation, the soul went forth to commence the journey and highway of the spirit, which is that of the advanced, which, by another name, is called the Road of Illumination or of Infused Contemplation, whereby God, of His own free will, proceeds to nourish and re-mold her unimpeded by any mental disquisition or active help, or industry on the part of the soul herself. Such is, as we have said, the night and purgation of the sense. The which, in those who are afterwards destined to enter upon the next more grievous night of the spirit, in order to pass to the divine union of love with God, (for it is not a passage that all go through, but restricted to exceeding few), is usually accompanied by grave sensitive trials and temptations which last a long time, although longer in the case of some than of others; for, to some is sent the angel of Satan, which is the spirit of fornication, to lash their senses with abominable and strenuous temptations, and trouble the mind with hideous thoughts, and images so clearly shadowed forth by the imagination, that it is at times more unendurable than death itself.

To this sad night is added, at other times, the spirit of blasphemy, the which crosses the current of all their ideas and thoughts with intolerable blasphemies, at times, so forcibly suggested to the imagination, that they are almost constrained to give them utterance, which is, to them, a most grave cross.

At other times they are tormented by another abominable spirit called by Isaiah *Spiritus vertiginis.*[25] The which darkens their senses after such a fashion as to fill them with a thousand scruples and perplexities, which appear to them so involved and intricate that they can never satisfy themselves in anything, nor stay their faltering judgment upon any prop of counsel or thought: the which is one of the gravest stings and horrors of this night, and next neighbor to what the soul suffers in the spiritual night.

These storms and trials God sends, as a rule, in this night and sensitive purgation, to those he intends to place afterwards in the next (although not all pass thither), so that being thus chastised and buffeted, they may gradually practice, dispose and harden the senses and powers to receive the Union of Wisdom they shall therein receive. For, if the soul is not tempted, tried and proved by temptations and trials, she cannot bring her senses into the harbor of Divine Wisdom. Wherefore said the Preacher: *Qui non est tentatus, quid scit? Qui non est expertus, pauca recognoscit.*[26] He who is not tempted, what knoweth he? And he who is not proved, what things doth he recognize? To the which truth Jeremiah well testifies, when he says: Castigaste me, *et eruditus sum.*[27] Thou chastenedst me, O Lord, and I was instructed. And the most appropriate manner of this chastisement, in order to enter into Wisdom, are the interior trials and conflicts that we here describe: forasmuch as they consist of those which most thoroughly purge the sense of all the delights and consolations whereto her natural frailty disposed her, and wherein, in very truth, the soul is humbled to the end that she may afterwards be exalted.

But as to the time the soul is held in this fast and penance of the sense, it can in no way, with certainty, be fixed; for all do not undergo the like discipline nor the same temptations, for this is a measure meted out by the Will of God, according as the imperfections to be purged less or more; and also, conformably to the grade of

Union of Love whereto God wills to raise her, so will He humble her the more or less intensely, or for a longer or shorter period. Those who have more capacity and strength for endurance, He purges with greater intensity and speed. For, as to the very feeble, He guides them through this night most intermittently, suiting their temptations to their weakness and makes the night to last much longer; constantly administering refreshment to the senses, so as to encourage and prevent them from turning back, and these arrive late at the purity of affection in this life, and some never. For they are neither well within the night, nor well outside of it; because, although they do not ascend higher, there are moments and days when God, in order to keep them in humility and the knowledge of themselves, proves and practices them in these drynesses and temptations, and helps them with His comfort: and at other times He does this for long intervals together, lest, losing heart, they turn back to seek the consolation of the world. With souls still weaker, God proceeds in other manner; constantly disappearing and hiding Himself from sight, in order to practice them in His love; for unless He turned away from them they would not learn to draw close to Him. But souls, whose high destiny it is to pass to so blessed and exalted a state as is the union of love, however rapidly God may lead them, continue, as a rule, in these aridnesses for a considerable time, as experience shews. Concluding, then, this book, let us begin to treat of the second night.

BOOK II

Wherein Discourse is Made of the Most Secret Purgation, Which is the Second Night of the Spirit[1]

NOT AT ONCE, UPON ISSUING FROM THE ARIDNESSES AND CONFLICTS OF the first purgation and night of the sense, doth God place the soul he intends to lead higher, in the union of love; rather, as a rule, long periods and years intervene, during which the soul, having issued forth from the initial stages proper to beginners, is practiced by His Majesty in those of the advanced in the union of love. Wherein (like one who hath escaped from a narrow prison), she proceeds with far greater liberty and interior satisfaction in the things of God, and receives more abundant and interior delight than she did at first, before she entered into this said night, the imagination and faculties being no longer, as before, fastened down to the disquisitions of meditation and mental effort. For, soon, with the utmost ease, she finds a most serene and loving contemplation and spiritual savor, free from all intellectual labor. Although, as the purgation of the spirit is not yet thoroughly accomplished (for the chief part is still amissing, which is the purgation of the intellect, without which, by reason of the communication that exists between the one part and the other, seeing that they form one subject); neither is the sensitive purgation, however searching it may have been, so perfected and finished as to be entirely free from certain aridnesses, darknesses, and conflicts, at times more intense than those she previously experienced, which are, as it were, the presages and heralds of the approaching night of the spirit, although these are not lasting, as shall be the night that awaits her. For having endured an interval, or intervals or days of this night or tempest, she again returns to her accustomed serenity; and after this fashion doth God proceed to purge certain souls which are not destined to aspire to so lofty a degree of love as others, by plunging them, for a space and intermittently, into this night of contemplation or spiritual purgation, making the shadows of night to darken over them, or bringing them forth into the light of dawn alternately; so that the words of David may be fulfilled, that He sends His crystal, that is, His contemplation, like morsels: *Mittit crystallums suum sicut buccellas.*[2] Although these morsels of dark contemplation are never so intense as is the darkness of this fearsome night of contemplation we are about to speak of, wherein God plunges the soul, of set purpose, to guide her to the Divine union.

This savor, then, and interior delight we speak of, which those who are advanced find and enjoy with abundance and ease within their spirit, is imparted to them far more abundantly than before, overflowing thence into the senses more than it did before this sensible purgation. Since, forasmuch as the spirit is now purer, it can taste the delights of the spirit with greater ease and after its own fashion. And as, in short, this sensitive part of the soul is weak and incapable of the strong things of the spirit, hence it is that these progressives, by reason of this spiritual communication which takes place with the sensitive part, suffer from great weakness, debility, and fatigue of stomach, and consequently fatigue of mind. For, as says the Wise Man, *Corpus enim, quod corrumpitur, aggravat animam.*[3] The corrupt body oppresses the soul. Hence it is that the communications bestowed on these can neither be very strong nor rigidly intense, nor very spiritual, as they must of necessity be for the Divine Union with God, by reason of the weakness and corruption of the sensuality which shares therein. And, hence, arise ecstasies and transports and dislocations of the bones, which always happen when the communications are

not absolutely spiritual; that is, to the spirit only, as are those
bestowed on the perfected, who have been, at length, purified
in the second night of the spirit, in whom these ecstasies and bodily
torments now cease, allowing them to rejoice in liberty of spirit,
free from all clouding over or transport of the sense. And in order
to shew the necessity such as these are under to enter into this night
of the spirit, we shall now point out some imperfections and dangers
which these progressives incur.

OF SOME IMPERFECTIONS ENTERTAINED BY PROGRESSIVES

These progressives labor under two kinds of imperfections, some
habitual, others actual: the habitual are the imperfect tendencies and
habits which, like roots, have been left behind still fixed in the spirit,
where the purgation of the sense could not reach. Whereof the purgation differs from the previous one, as do the roots from the boughs,
or the cleansing of a freshly made stain from one already established
for some time. For, as we have said, the purgation of the sense alone
is the door and basis of contemplation for that of the spirit, and it is
better to reconcile the sense to the spirit, than to unite the spirit with
God. But, nevertheless, the stains of the old Adam still cling to the
spirit, although it is blind and cannot see them: the which if they
are not made to yield to the soap and strong lye of the purgation of
this night, the spirit shall have no power to attain to the purity of the
Divine Union.

These also labor under the *hebetudo mentis* and natural stupidity
which each man contracts through sin, and distraction and exteriority
of spirit, all which must be illuminated, clarified, and kept from stray-
ing by the punishment and conflict of this night. All who have not
emerged from this imperfect state of progress contract these habitual
imperfections; the which cannot exist side by side with the perfect
stage of union by love with God.

As to actual imperfections, all do not incur them after the like
fashion; but certain of these, as they carry their spiritual gifts so
much on the surface and so amenable to the influence of the senses,
fall into various difficulties and perils whereof we spoke at the

beginning. For, as they find so many communications and perceptions showered upon the sense and spirit, wherein they often see
imaginary and spiritual visions (for all this, together with other pleasurable sensations, happens to many of these in this stage wherein the
devil and their own fancy, most generally, play fantastic tricks upon
the soul), and as the devil is wont with such delight to imprint upon,
and suggest to, the soul, the said perceptions and sensations, he
dazzles and deceives her with the utmost ease, as she is not suffi-
ciently cautious to resign herself to God and make a determined
fight against all these visions and sensations. For, now the devil
makes them give credence to many vain visions and false prophe-
cies, and does his best to make them think that God and the Saints
hold converse with them, and ofttimes they believe in the wild
vagaries of their fancy. In this stage, the devil is wont to fill them
with presumption and pride, and allured by vanity and arrogance,
they allow themselves to be seen of others in exterior actions which
bear aspect of sanctity, such as ecstasies and other displays. Thus
they wax bold against God, losing Holy fear which is the key and
Tabernacle of all virtue; and in certain of these people so greatly do
falsehoods and deceptions increase and multiply, and so hardened do they get therein, that their return to the pure road of virtue
and true spirit is extremely doubtful. Into the which basenesses they
end by falling, by abandoning themselves with too much confidence
to spiritual cognitions and sensations, when they begin to make
progress on the spiritual road. So much still remains to be said of
the imperfections of these people, and as to how they are the more
incurable, forasmuch as they account them of a more spiritual nature
than their previous experiences, that I am fain to leave the subject.
I only repeat (so as more strenuously to urge upon him who would
fain rise higher, the necessity there is for the spiritual night, which
is purgation), that, for the most part, none of these progressives,
despite his utmost care, fails to entertain many of these natural
tendencies and habits of imperfection; wherefrom, as we have said,
it is first necessary to be purified if we would pass to Divine Union.
And, furthermore, besides that we have said above, to wit, that,

forasmuch as the lower part still participates in these spiritual communications, they cannot be so intense, pure, and vigorous as is requisite for the desired union: therefore, in order to attain thereto, the soul must enter into the second night of the spirit, where absolutely denuding the sense and spirit from all these cognitions and delightful savors, she is made to accomplish her journey in the darkness of absolute Faith, which is the proper and adequate means whereby the soul is made one with God, as Hosea declares: *Sponsabo te mihi in fide.*[4] I will join thee to me in marriage, that is, I will join thee to myself in Faith.

PREPARATION FOR WHAT FOLLOWS

These progressives, then, having experienced these sweet communications during the period they have, at length, with so much difficulty, won through; to the end that the sensitive part being thus allured and having acquired a zest for the spiritual delight which emanated from the spirit, may be incorporated and made one with it, each being fed after its own fashion with the same spiritual meat, and out of the same bowl of a single substance and subject; so that they, being thus, in some sort, united and welded into one, may be disposed to suffer the harsh and cruel purgation of the spirit which awaits them; wherein these two parts of the soul, spiritual and sensitive, must be thoroughly purged; because, one is never entirely purged without the other, since the conclusive purging for the sense is when, in good earnest, that of the spirit commences. Whence, we should, and must, call the night of the sense we have spoken of, a certain shaping afresh and bridling in of the appetite, rather than a purgation. The reason is, because all imperfections and unruliness of the sensitive part have their strength and root in the spirit; and so, until evil habits are purged out, it is impossible thoroughly to purge away its rebellions and perversities. Whence, in this second night that follows, both parts are purged conjointly, for this is the object wherefore it was necessary to undergo the reformation of the first night, and to issue into the fair weather which it brought about; so that the sensitive part being joined with the spirit, they may both, in a certain manner, be purged and mutually undergo the sufferings of the next with greater valor and fortitude, which for so drastic and stubborn a purge is indeed most urgent: for, if the weakness of the inferior part has not already been reformed beforehand and acquired confidence in God through the sweet and pleasant converse it then enjoyed with Him, the physical constitution would have neither strength nor disposition to suffer it.

Wherefore, the converse and dealings which these progressives hold with God are of an extremely material nature, because the gold of the spirit has not yet been purified and polished, on which account they still think of God like children, and know and perceive God like children, as says St. Paul: *Cùm essem parvulus, loquebar ut parvulus, sapiebam ut parvulus, cogitabam ut parvulus.*[5] The reason being that they have not reached perfection, which is the union of love with God, by which union having at length arrived, as it were, at man's estate, their spirit works magnificent operations, their acts and powers having now become more Divine than human, as shall presently be said: God having willed to strip them, in very truth, of this old Adam, and clothe them with the new, which, in order to God, is created in the newness of sense, as saith the Apostle: *Et induite novum hominem, qui secundùm Deum creatus est.*[6] And in another place: *Reformamini in novitate sensus vestri;*[7] he strips them of the powers and affections and senses, spiritual as well as sensible, interior as well as exterior, leaving the mind in darkness, and the Will stranded, and the memory void, and the desires of the soul in profound distress, bitterness, and conflict, depriving her of the sense and pleasure which she before felt in spiritual favors, so that this privation shall be one of the conditions essential for the spirit, in order that the spiritual form of the spirit, which is the union of love, may be infused into, and united with, it. All which the Lord works on the soul by means of an absolute and obscure contemplation, as she herself declares in the first song. The which, although it is explained at the beginning of the first night of the sense, the soul chiefly intends it to apply to this second night of the spirit, inasmuch as it is the principal agent in bringing about her purification. And so, in this sense and to this end, we shall once more write it down and proceed with our exposition.

THE FIRST SONG IS SET DOWN TOGETHER WITH THE EXPOSITION THEREOF

> Into the strange dark night
> With longing flaming into love,
> Oh happy chance!
> I went, no eye to note,
> My house being hushed in sleep.

If we now take the meaning of this song to be purgation, contemplation, or nakedness or poverty of spirit, for, with scarce any difference,
they amount to one and the same thing, we may expound it after the
manner following, and say that the soul sings thus: in poverty and
bereft of all cognitions of my soul, that is, in the darkness of my understanding and constriction of my will, in affliction and agony of
memory, being left in utter darkness to the sole guidance of Faith,
which of herself is darkest night for the said natural powers, my will
alone being touched with grief, mourning, and longing after the love
of God, I went forth from out of myself; that is, from my base material
mode of understanding, and for my weak capacity for love, and from
my poverty-stricken and grovelling fashion of tasting God, neither
sensuality nor the devil being able to bar the road. The which, for me,
was a great happiness, and of blissful augury; for when I had made an
end of routing out, exterminating and silencing the powers, passions
and affections of my soul, wherewith after a base and miserable fashion I had known and tasted of God, I went forth from out the converse
and scanty exercises related, to the operations of, and converse with,
God. That is to say, my understanding escaped from itself, being from
human, transmuted into Divine; because, being united with God by
means of this purgation, it no longer perceives in the same limited
and imperfect way as before, but by the Divine Wisdom wherewith it
has been united. And my will escaped from itself, making itself Divine:
for, since it has now become one with Divine love, it loves no longer
with the cribbed and confined strength and vigor as of yore, but with
the passionate strength and purity of the Divine Spirit; and so, the will
works no longer in respect of God after human fashion; in exactly the
same way as the memory is absolutely changed into eternal reflections

and perceptions of glory. And finally, every energy and passion of the Soul by means of this night and the purgation of the old Adam are born afresh into Divine harmonies and delights.

FIRST IS SET DOWN THE FIRST LINE, AND AFTERWARDS BEGINS THE EXPOSITION AS TO HOW THIS DARK CONTEMPLATION IS NOT ONLY NIGHT FOR THE SOUL, BUT ALSO PAIN AND TORMENT

IN A DARK NIGHT

This dark night is an influence from God upon the soul, which purges her of her ignorance and habitual imperfections, natural and spiritual, and is styled by contemplatives, infused contemplation or mythical theology, wherein God teaches the soul in secret, and instructs her in the perfect love, all act on her part being limited to fixing her attention lovingly on God, listening to His voice and receiving the light He sends, without knowing what manner of thing this infused contemplation is. Inasmuch as it is the benignant Wisdom of God, the which works particular effects upon the soul; for, by purging and illuminating her, it disposes her for the union of love with God, where this most loving Wisdom herself, which purges the spirits of the blessed, by shining on them in their brightness, is she who now purges the soul and illuminates her.

But the doubt presents itself, why does the soul apply such a term as dark night to the Divine light which, as we say, illuminates and purges her of her blindness? Whereto it is answered, that in respect of two considerations, this Divine Wisdom is not only night and darkness for the soul, but also pain and torment. The first is by reason of the altitude of the Divine Wisdom, which exceeds the comprehension of the soul, and is therefore dark as night to her. The second, because of her own baseness and impurity, and therefore it is to her noisome and grievous, and also dark. In order to prove the first, we must surmise a certain doctrine of the Philosopher, who says, that inasmuch as Divine things are of themselves more clear and evident, so much the more are they darkness to, and naturally hidden from, the soul. In the same way the pupil of an owl sees less and becomes the more contracted in the light, the more brilliant it is, and the more boldly she looks into the eye of the sun, the more is her power of vision darkened, if not entirely extinguished, the light being too excessive for her weakness. Hence, when this Divine Light of Contemplation seizes upon the soul which, as yet, is not entirely illustrated and illuminated, it shrouds her in spiritual darkness, for not only does it transcend her powers, but also obscures and deprives her of the action of her natural intelligence. And this is the cause why San Dionysius and other mystic theologians call this infused contemplation a ray of darkness; this is to say, for the non-illuminated and unpurged soul, because the natural strength of the intellect is vanquished by its supernatural and stupendous light, and bereft of the action and the intellectual energy which belongs to it. Wherefore David also said: *Nubes, et caligo in circuitu ejus.*[8] That darkness and cloud surrounds and encompasses God: not because it is actually so, but by reason of our weak perceptions, which, unable to reach heights so sublime, are confounded and blinded by so immense a light. Wherefore David himself declared so, saying: *Prae fulgore in conspectu ejus nubes transierunt.*[9] The thick clouds were pierced by reason of the great splendor of His presence; that is to say, between God and our mind. And this is the reason, because, when God emanates from Himself to the soul which is not yet transformed, this translucent ray of His secret Wisdom envelops the understanding in deep clouds. And that this obscure contemplation is, also, at first, painful to the soul, is evident; for, as this Divine infused contemplation possesses many excellencies supremely noble, and the soul which receives them, as she is not yet fully purged, is held back by many miseries; hence it is, that as it is impossible for one subject to contain two opposites, the soul, perforce, must suffer pain and agony, she being the substance in which these two opposites are contained, which struggle one against the other, by reason of the purgation from the imperfections of the soul, which is accomplished through this contemplation. The which we will prove by induction in manner following: in respect of the first, since the light and wisdom of this contemplation is extremely clear and pure, and the soul whereon it seizes, dark and impure, hence it is, that it is most painful to her to receive it, like as when the eyes, if they are bleared and diseased, are hurt and injured by the striking on them of a radiant light; and this agony of the soul, on account of her impurity, is immense when, in very truth, this Divine Light reverberates upon her, for when this pure light shines upon her, to the end of expelling her impurities, she feels herself so impure and wretched that it seems to her that God is against her, and that she has become God's enemy. The which is such torture and affliction to the soul (since now, indeed, it seems to her that God has cast her off), that one of the trials Job felt most keenly when God placed him in this exercise, was this saying: *Quare posuisti me contrarium tibi, et factus sum mihimetipsi gravis?*[10] Why hast thou made me Thy enemy, and I am a weight and burden to myself? For as the soul now clearly sees her own impurity by means of this clear and pure light (although she is in darkness), she clearly perceives that she is unworthy of God and of all creatures whatsoever.

And what torments her most is the fear that she will never be worthy, and that all her gains are forever destroyed. The cause of this is the profound immersion the mind is plunged into in the knowledge and recognition of its own evilness and baseness. For, now, this Divine and obscure light sets it all before her eyes, that she may clearly see that, of herself, she can have nothing else. We may take this to be the meaning of this text of David, where he says: *Propter iniquitatem corripuisti hominem: et tabescere fecisti sicut araneam animam ejus.*[11] In respect of his iniquity didst thou chastise man, and madest his soul to consume even as the spider tears out her own bowels. The second way wherein the soul is afflicted, is by reason of her physical and spiritual weakness; for as this Divine contemplation seizes upon the soul with a certain force, to the end that it may gradually fortify and tame her, so deeply is she afflicted in her weakness that she almost swoons; particularly when, sometimes, it seizes upon her with somewhat greater force; because the sense and spirit, like as they lay crushed beneath some immense, mysterious weight, suffer torments and agony so great, that they would fain choose death itself as being a mitigation of their pain. The which having been experienced by the Holy Job, he said: *Nolo multa fortitudine contendat mecum, ne magnitudinis suæ mole me premat.*[12] I beseech Him not to deal with me in His great strength, that I be not crushed under the weight of His greatness.

For in the strength of this weight and oppression, the soul feels herself so far from being in favor, that it seems to her, as indeed it is, that even that wherein she was wont to find some support, has failed her with the rest, and that there is no one to take compassion on her. Which also is the meaning of the words of Job: *Miseremini mei, miseremini mei, saltem vos, amici mei, quia manus Domini tetigit me.*[13] Take compassion on me, have compassion on me, at least, oh you, my friends! Because the hand of the Lord has touched me. A mighty marvelous and pitiful thing, that the weakness and impurity of the soul should be so great, that the hand of the Lord, being of itself so benignant and so tender, she finds it now so harsh and heavy, although it be not laid nor placed upon her heavily, only touches her most gently, and this in mercy, since it does so in order to shower upon her favors and not chastisement.

OF OTHER KINDS OF TORMENT THE SOUL SUFFERS IN THIS NIGHT

The third manner of passion and agony that the soul now suffers, is by reason of other two extremes, to wit, the Divine and the Human, which now become one. The Divine is this contemplative purgation, and the Human is the substance of the soul. For, as the Divine seizes upon her to the end that she may be seasoned and renewed so as to be made Divine, and stripped naked of the habitual propensities and properties of the old Adam, wherewith she is still closely joined, cemented and assimilated, after such a fashion does it grind and disintegrate her, sucking her down into darkness so profound, that she feels herself consumed and melted before the sight and aspect of her basenesses, in a cruel death of the spirit; like as she were swallowed up in the darksome belly of some monster and felt herself being crunched within its jaws, and suffers the same agonies as Jonah, in the belly of the whale. For, even so must she dwell in this sepulchre of darkest death, if she would awake to the spiritual resurrection that awaits her. The manner of this passion and grief, although in good truth, it is beyond conception, is described by David when he says: *Circumdederunt me dolores mortis—dolores inferni circumdederunt me—in tribulatione mea invocavi Domimum, et ad Deum meum clamavi.*[14] The pains of death encompassed me, I was surrounded by the horrors of hell, I cried aloud in my anguish. But what this grief-stricken soul feels most of all, is the thought that God has most certainly forsaken her, and that in His loathing of her, He has cast her into the abyss of darkness, which is, for her, a grievous and pitiable suffering to believe that God has forsaken her. The which, also, David, in a like case, feeling deeply, says: *Sicut vulnerati dormientes in sepulchris, quorum non es memor amplius: et ipsi de manu tua repulsi sunt: posuerunt me in loco inferiori, in tenebrosis, et in umbra mortis: super me confirmatus est furor tuus: et omnes fluctus tuos induxisti super me.*[15] Like as wounded men lie dead in sepulchres, from whom Thou hast lifted Thy hand, and of whom Thou hast no more memory: so placed they me in the deep and nethermost lake, in the darkness and shadow of death, and, therefore, Thy anger is confirmed upon me, and all Thy waves Thou lettedst loose upon me. For, truly, when this purgative contemplation constrains, the soul feels the shadow of death and the groans and tortures of Hell, as if she saw them bodily before her, for Hell to her consists in feeling herself forsaken of God, and chastised and flung aside, and that He is outraged and wrathful, for all this she suffers now; and furthermore, she is overcome by a direful terror that it is forever. And she is haunted by this same sense of being forsaken and despised of all created people and things, particularly of her friends. For this reason it is that David goes on to say: *Longe feciste notos meos à me: posuerunt me abominationem sibi.*[16] Thou didst turn away my friends and acquaintances from me, they held me for an abomination. To all which, as one who had likewise experienced it bodily and spiritually, Jonas testifies, in the following words: *Projecisti me in profundum in corde maris, et flumen circumdedit me: omnes gurgites tui, et fluctus tui super me transierunt. Et ego dixi: abjectus sum à conspectu oculorum tuorum: verumtamèn rursus videbo templum. Sanctum tuum: circumdederunt me aquæ usque ad animam: abyssus vallavit me, pelagus operuit caput meum. Ad extrema montium descendi: terræ vectes concluserunt me in aeternum.*[17] Thou didst cast me into the deep, into the heart of the sea, and the flood surrounded me; all its gulfs and waves passed over me, and I said: I am cast out from the presence of Thy eyes; but I shall once more see Thy Holy Temple (the which he says, because the soul is now purified by God to perceive it): the waters surrounded me, yea, to my very soul, the abyss girt me about, the sea covered my head, I descended to the roots of the mountains; the bolts of the earth shut on me forever. By which bolts are here meant the imperfections of the soul, which hinder her from enjoying this delightful contemplation.

A further excellency of this dark contemplation begets in the soul a fourth kind of grief, which is the Majesty and Grandeur of God, which gives rise in her to the other extreme therein contained, of her own intimate poverty and wretchedness; the which is one of the chiefest tortures she suffers in this purgation. For, she feels within herself a profound void and utter dearth of the three kinds of wealth which are ordered for her enjoyment, which are: temporal, physical, and spiritual; and she sees herself plunged into the contrary evils, to wit: miserable trifles of imperfections, aridnesses and emptinesses of the perceptions of the faculties, and desolation of the spirit in darkness. For, inasmuch as God now purges the soul of her spiritual as well as her sensitive substance, of her interior as of her exterior powers, it is necessary that she be placed in emptiness and poverty and desertion on all sides, and be left parched, void, and empty and in darkness. For the sensitive part is purified by dryness, and the intellectual powers in the void of their cognitions, and the spirit in thick darkness. All which God effects by means of this obscure contemplation; wherein, not only does the soul suffer the void and suspension of these her usual supports and perceptions, which is a kind of suffering most agonizing (like as if a person were hung or suspended in the air, so that he could not breathe) but he also purges her, destroying or voiding or consuming therein (like as fire works on the rust and tarnish of metals), from all the affections and imperfect habits she has contracted throughout her life. And, forasmuch as they are deeply rooted in her, she suffers grave restlessness and interior torture, beside the said poverty, and physical and mental void. In order that the utterance of Ezekiel be here fulfilled, where he says: *Congere ossa, quæ igne succendam: consumentur carnes, et coquetur universa compositio, et ossa tabescent.*[18] I will gather together the bones, and I will kindle them into fire, the flesh shall be consumed, and the whole mass seethed, and the bones shall crumble into dust. Whereby is shewn the torture the soul suffers in respect of the emptiness and poverty she is in as to the sensitive and spiritual parts. And respecting this, he goes on to say: *Pone quoque eam super prunas vacuam, ut incalescat, et liquefiat æs ejus: et confletur in medio ejus inquinamentum ejus, et consumatur rubigo ejus.*[19] Cast her likewise, empty as she is, upon the burning coals, so that she may wax hot and her hardness be melted, and her foulness consumed in the midst of her, and her rust cleansed. Wherein is shewn the passionate agony the soul endures in the purgation of the fire of this contemplation: for, as the prophet says here, that in order to purify and cleanse away the rust of the affections which remain in the center of the soul, it is necessary that she herself, to a certain extent, should cooperate in this self-annihilation and disintegration, in so far as these passions and imperfections have become a part of her. Whence, in this furnace the soul is purified like as gold in the crucible, as the Wise Man says: *Tamquam aurum in fornace probavit illos.*[20] She feels this fearful breaking up in the innermost part of her with excessive sadness, wherein she feels herself, as it were, about to give up the ghost. As may be seen in what David says of himself in a like case, calling upon God in these words: *Salvum ne fac Deus, quoniam intraverunt usque ad animam meam. Infixus sum in limo profundi: et non est substantia: veni in altitudinem maris: et tempestas demersit me: laboravi clamans raucæ factæ sunt fauces meæ: defecerunt oculi mei, dum spero in Deum meum.*[21] Save me, O Lord, because the waters have entered even unto my soul; I am stuck fast in the mire of the deep, and I can find no stay; I sought the depths of the sea, and the tempest swallowed me up; I called aloud in my anguish, my throat waxed hoarse, my eyes closed even whilst I wait upon my God. Here God humiliates the soul profoundly to exalt her greatly afterwards, and were He not to bid this grief when it swells within the soul, quickly to be still, in a very few days she must forsake the body; but the moments, wherein it makes itself felt in its most intense vitality, are intermittent. The which is sometimes so keen and piercing, that the soul bethinks her that she sees Hell and perdition open before her. For, of such as these, are they who, in very truth, go down to Hell in life, and are purged in this world as if in the purgatory of the next; for this purgation, being a purgation from sins, however venial they may be, is like to that which must be accomplished there. And so the soul which passes through this purification and is left thoroughly purged, either does not enter into Hades, or stays not long there, for, in one hour of this earthly purgatory, she derives more benefit than in many there.

The afflictions and conflicts of the will are now, also, infinite, and of such a nature that, sometimes, they transfix the soul with the sudden memory of the evil wherein she sees herself, and the uncertainty of the remedy. And to this is added the memory of former prosperity; for these souls, when they enter into this night, have, as a rule, been accustomed to have many delights in God and to do Him great service, and this grieves them the more, to see that they are become strangers to this grace, and that they can no longer enter therein. This Job, as one who had experience thereof, also says, in these words: *Ego ille quondam opulentus repentè contritus sum: tenuit cervicem meam, confregit me, et posuit me sibi quasi in signum. Circumdedit me lanceis suis, convulneravit lumbos meos non pepercit, et effudit in terra viscera mea. Concidit me vulnere super vulnus, irruit in me quasi gigas. Saccum consui super cutem meam, et operui cinere carnem meam. Facies mea intumuit à fletu, et palpebræ meæ caligaverunt.*[22] I who am he who was once wealthy and rich, of a sudden am I undone and contrite; He seized me by the nape of the neck, He ground me, and set me as His mark to shoot at me, He surrounded me with His spears, He wounded me in every part of my loins, He pardoned not, He poured out my bowels on the ground, He broke me, and added wounds to wounds; He seized me, as it were, a powerful giant, I sewed a sack upon my skin, and I covered my flesh with ashes; my face is swollen with weeping and my eyes are blinded. Such and so great are the torments of this night, and so many are the authorities furnished by the Scriptures, which might be quoted in this connection, that were we to set them down, time and strength would fail us; for, without doubt, all we can say, falls short; from the quotations already given, some idea may be formed thereof. And to bring this line to an end, and set forth what this night is in the soul, I will repeat what Jeremiah thinks thereof, as follows:

Ego vir videns paupertatem meam in virga indignationis ejus. Me minavit, et adduxit in tenebras, et non in lucem. Tantum in me vertit, et convertit manum suam tota die. Vetustam fecit pellém meam, et carnem meam, contrivit ossa mea. Œdificavit in gyro meo, et circumdedit me felle, et labore. In tenebrosis collocavit me, quasi mortuos sempiternos. Circumædificovit adversùm me, ut non egrediar: aggravavit compedem meum. Sed et cùm clamavero, et rogavero, exclusit orationem meam. Conclusit vias meas lapidibus quadris, semitas meas subvertit. Ursus insidians factus est mihi, leo in absconditis. Semitas meas subvertit, et confregit me: posuit me desolatam. Tetendit arcum suum, et posuit me quasi signum ad sagittam. Misit in renibus meis filias pharetræ suæ. Factus sum in derisum omni populo meo, canticum eorum tota die. Replevit me amaritudinibus, inebriavit me absynthio, et fregit ad numerum dentes meos, cibavit me, cinere. Et repulsa est à pace anima mea, oblitus sum bonorum, et dixi: Periit finis meus, et spes mea à Domino. Recordare paupertatis, et transgressionis meæ, absynthii, et fellis: Memoria memor ero, et tabescet in me anima mea.[23]

I am a man who sees my vileness in the rod of his indignation; He has threatened me and brought me into darkness, and not to light. He has turned and directed His hand upon me all day long, He made my skin and my flesh old, He ground my bones into dust: He besieged me round about, and surrounded me with gall and affliction; He placed me in darkness, as those dead forever. He laid His siege against me round about, so that I might not escape, He made fast my bonds. And likewise, when I have called and besought Him, He has excluded my prayer. He has barred up my ways and issues with square stones, He has confounded my steps. He posted His spies to lie in wait for me like a lion in his den. He confounded and broke me into bits, He made me to be forsaken; He stretched His bow, and made me the mark of His

arrow. He pierced my bowels with the daughters of His quiver. I am
made a mockery to all people, a laughing stock, and a byeword to
them all day long. He has filled me with bitterness, He has made me
drunk with wormwood. He hath broken my teeth one by one, He fed
me with ashes. My soul is cast out from peace, I am forgotten of all
good. As I said, My end is brought to nought and finished, also my
pretension and hope of the Lord. Remember my misery and my abundance, the wormwood and the gall. I must remember me as long as my
memory endureth, and my soul shall melt for sorrow within me.

All these lamentations Jeremiah makes over these tortures and
conflicts, wherein he paints most vividly, the passions of the soul
wherein she is plunged by this purgation and spiritual night. Hence it
behoves us to have great compassion on the soul whom God sets in
this fearful and horrible night. For although exceeding happiness
accrues to her in respect of the great mercies which are to flow to her
therefrom, when, as says Job, God shall raise up in the soul, from darkness the profoundest benefits, and the shadow of death shall generate
light; *Qui revelat profunda de tenebris, et producit in lucem umbram mortis.*[24]
So that, as David says, its light shall become as great as was the darkness: *Sicut tenebræ ejus, ita et lumen ejus:*[25] nevertheless, such is the
unfathomable torture she continues to suffer, and the great uncertainty she feels of her remedy, as it seems to her (as the prophet
here says), that her sufferings can never end, thinking as David likewise says: *Collocavit me in obscuris sicut mortuos sæculi,*[26] that God has
placed her in a darkness as of those that have been long dead, and for
this has He plunged her spirit within her into such anguish, and troubled her heart with such affliction; she deserves, indeed, the greatest
grief and pity. For to this is added that she cannot, owing to the
solitude and desolation this night produces in her, find comfort or
support in any teaching nor in any spiritual master. For however much
he may try to shew her, by many ways, how great the reasons she
has for rejoicing, in respect of the mercies concealed within these
tortures, she may not believe it. For, as she is so immersed and
absorbed in this passionate sorrow for her own evil doings wherein she
so clearly sees her vileness, she thinks that, as others do not see, what
she sees and feels, they speak from lack of apprehension, and instead

of comfort, rather doth she receive fresh grief, thinking that this is no remedy for her hurt, and, truly, she is right. For until the Lord makes an end of purging her, after the fashion He deigns to appoint, no means nor remedy will serve or avail to mitigate her grief. The more especially as the soul can do as little in this condition of terror as he who, bound hand and foot, is cast into a dark dungeon, unable to move or see, or to perceive any help from above or below, until, in this purgation the spirit is softened, humbled, and purified, and becomes so refined, simple, and rarified, as to be enabled to become one with the spirit of God, according to the degree of union of love His mercy vouchsafes to concede; for, in accordance with this, is the purgation more or less severe, or for a longer or shorter time. But, if it is to be a durable and lasting matter, howsoever great its severity, it endures for some years; it being understood that, during them, there are intermissions and alleviations, in which by the dispensation of God, this obscure contemplation ceases to afflict the soul after a purgative mode and fashion, but comes to her illuminatively and lovingly, wherein, like a prisoner escaped from so noisome a dungeon and bondage, and set in the refreshment of space and liberty, she tastes and feels to the full, great suavity of peace and loving friendship with God with easy abundance of spiritual intercourse. The which is to the soul a sign of the salvation that the said purgation is working in her, and a presage of the abundance that awaits her. And this even, at times, to such a degree, that at last the soul thinks that all her trials are fairly ended. For spiritual things in the soul are of this nature, when they are most purely spiritual; that when her trials return, she thinks that she shall never escape therefrom, and that now, indeed, there is an end to all her treasures, as has been seen from the passages already quoted; and when her spiritual treasures are renewed, she likewise thinks that her labors are over, and that her treasures will never again fail her, like David who, seeing himself in a like case, confessed it saying: *Ego autem dixi in abundantia mea, non movebor in æternum.*[27] I said in my abundance: henceforth I shall never be moved. And this befalls, because the actual, mental possession of one contrary, of itself stirs up the actual possession of, and sorrow for, the other contrary; the which does not so much affect the sensitive part of the soul, because its apprehension is weak. But be it as it may, if the spirit is not yet thoroughly purged and cleansed of the tendencies contracted by the inferior part, although it has acquired greater consistency and firmness; but, forasmuch as it is still affected by them, so is it subject to greater suffering, like as we see that David was afterwards changed by experiencing great hurt and sorrow, although in the season of his abundance he had thought and said that he would never be moved. So the soul, as then she sees herself supported with this abundance of spiritual wealth, not being able to perceive the root of imperfection and impurity that still remains, thinks that her trials are ended. But this thought occurs but seldom; for, until the spiritual purification is completed, her sweet intercourse with God is very seldom so abundant as to hide the root left behind, in such a way that it does not make itself perceptible to her in her most inward part, as somewhat, I know not what, amissing, or still to be accomplished, which does not allow her to rejoice to the full in this alleviation, feeling there within, as it were, an enemy, who, although apparently quiescent and asleep, is to be feared lest he should come back to life and play his former pranks. And so it is, that when the soul is most secure, he again swallows and absorbs her in another stage still more cruel, dark, and pitiful than the last, the which shall, peradventure, last another and a longer time than the first. And again, the soul ends by persuading herself that she is bereft for good of all her treasures. For her past experience of the former good she enjoyed after her first conflict, wherein she likewise thought that nought but suffering was in store for her, doth not suffice to shake her belief that in this second degree of affliction, all has, at length, come to an end, and shall not return, as it did before. For, as I say, this belief, so strongly rooted, is produced in the soul by the immediate apprehension of the mind, which extinguishes in her everything that can cause her joy. And thus, the soul set in this purgation, although it seems to her that she loves God and would give for Him a thousand lives (as is indeed the truth, for in these conflicts these souls love their God in desperate earnest); withal this is no mitigation of her torture, rather doth it increase her grief, for as she loves Him so entirely as to care for nothing else, yet as she perceives her own utter wretchedness, full of doubt and fear as to whether God loves her or not, and not being certain for the time being that she is worthy to be loved, but rather to be loathed, not only of Him, but of every creature forever, she mourns to see in herself reasons wherefore she deserves to be flung aside by Him she so ardently loves and desires.

OF OTHER WOES WHICH AFFLICT THE SOUL IN THIS STATE

In this state there is something else which greatly troubles and distresses the soul, and it is that, as this dark night deprives her of her powers and inclinations, she cannot, as before, raise her mind or affection to God, nor can she pray to Him, it seeming to her, as to Jeremiah, that God has placed a cloud before her eyes on purpose that no prayer of hers shall pierce it: *Opposuiste nubem tibi, ne transeat oratio.*[28] For this means what the Scripture we have quoted says: *Conclusit vias meas lapidibus quadris.*[29] He blocked my issues with square stones. And if sometimes she prays, it is with such dryness and want of fervor, that she thinks God does not hear her nor give heed, as the prophet also shews in the same text, saying: *Sed et cùm clamavero, et rogavero, exclusit orationem meam.*[30] When I cried out and besought Him, He shut out my prayer. In truth, as Jeremiah says, this is the time to bow down her mouth into the dust: *Ponet in pulvere os suum,*[31] and to suffer with patience her purgation. God Himself it is who is now working in the soul; therefore she herself can do nothing. Whence she can neither pray nor fix her attention to any purpose on the Divine matters she takes part in, anymore than she can, in any other matter appertaining to temporal things and intercourse; nor is this all, for ofttimes she is overtaken by such absences of mind, such profound lapses of memory, that for long intervals together, she is unconscious of what she did or thought, or what she is doing or is about to do, nor can she concentrate her attention, in spite of all her efforts, on anything she is engaged upon.

Forasmuch as not only, in this state, is the understanding purged of its imperfect knowledge and the will of its affections, but also the memory of its ideas and speculations, so must the soul, likewise, become dead to them all, so that what David says of himself in this purgation may be fulfilled: *Et ego ad nihilum redactus sum, et nescivi.*[32] I was brought to nought, and I knew not. The which extinction of knowledge extends to these dulnesses and lapses of memory, the which states of loss of consciousness and absences of mind are caused by the interior gathering inward of the faculties, and the total absorption of the soul in contemplation. For, in order that the soul and her powers may be disposed and Divinely attuned for the Divine Union of Love, it was needful that she with all her faculties should first be absorbed into this Divine and obscure spiritual light of contemplation, and be thus withdrawn from all affections and knowledge of the creature, the duration whereof is measured by its intensity. And so, the more purely and absolutely this Divine light shines upon the soul so much the more does it darken, and empty, and annihilate her in respect of her particular conceptions and affections, whether of things above or below. And likewise, when it shines upon her less clearly and purely, so much the less does it suspend her and the less obscure it is. For, it seems incredible to assert that the supernatural and Divine light darkens the soul the more, the more lucid and pure it is; and in so far as its translucency and purity is less, so is its obscurity.

The which we can the more fully understand if we consider the proof given above in the maxim of the philosopher, to wit, that supernatural things are so much the more obscure to our minds, inasmuch as of themselves, they are the more clear and evident. And so, when the ray of this sublime contemplation touches the soul with its light Divine, so in the same proportion as it transcends the natural capacity of the soul herself, doth it darken and deprive her of all her natural affections and conceptions, which before, by means of her physical enlightenment, she apprehended. Wherewith not only does it leave her in darkness, but likewise empty as regards her powers and appetites, spiritual as well as natural. For like as a ray of light, if it is pure and meets with no object in its course whence it is scattered or reverberated, is almost imperceptible, and is most clearly seen in its reverberation or reflection; so this spiritual light wherein the soul is steeped, by reason of its excessive purity, is not of itself so distinctly perceptible or visible; yet when it is shattered or reverberated from some object, that is, when anything specially relating to perfection is presented to the mind or it is called upon to judge and decide between what is false or true; it at once perceives and understands it with infinitely more clearness than before she passed through this darkness. And so precisely in the same way doth she know the spiritual light she possesses, which enables her to recognize with ease the imperfection that is placed before her: like as the ray is not of itself so clearly to be seen, yet if a hand or anything else intercepts its course, the hand is at once seen, and we know that the light of the sun was resting on it. Whence, in respect of the simplicity, purity, and all embracing nature of this spiritual light, untainted and unrestricted to any intelligible particular, natural or Divine (since, in regard to all these conceptions the powers of the soul are void and null), the soul knows and penetrates with an all embracing facility whatsoever earthly or celestial thing is placed before her; for which reason the Apostle said: *Spiritus enim omnia scrutator, etiam profunda Dei.*[33] For the spiritual man penetrateth all things, even to the depths of God. For it is of this all embracing and absolute Wisdom that the Holy Ghost speaks through the mouth of the Sage: *Attingit autem ubique propter suam munditiam.*[34] That it goeth where it listeth on account of its extreme purity: to wit, because it is not restricted to any intelligible particular or affection. And this is the property of the spirit, purged and emptied of all particular affections and intelligencies, for in this total absence of delight in, and lack of intellectual knowledge of, any particular, abiding in her emptiness, obscurity, and darkness, she embraces all things most powerfully so that therein the words of St. Paul may be mystically verified: *Nihil habentes, et omnia possidentes.*[35] For such is the blessedness due to a poverty of spirit so extreme.

WHEREFORE, ALTHOUGH THIS NIGHT CASTS DARKNESS OVER THE SPIRIT, IT DOES SO OF PURPOSE TO ILLUMINATE AND ENLIGHTEN IT

It remains, then, here to declare that this blissful night, although it casts the spirit into darkness, does so solely in order to enlighten it in all things; and although it humbles and abases it, it is solely in order to exalt and give it freedom; and although it impoverishes and empties it of all natural possessions and affections, it is solely to enable it to stretch Divinely forth to full enjoyment and delight in all things whether of heaven or earth, in the absolute possession of an all embracing liberty of spirit in all things. For, like as the elements, in order to be united in all bodily beings and compounds, must not be affected with any particular quality of color, smell, nor taste, so that all concur therein in all savors, odors, and colors, so must the spirit be simple, pure, and denuded of all manner of bodily affections and tendencies, whether actual or habitual, before she can converse with freedom with the vast expanse of the spirit of Divine Wisdom, wherein on account of her cleanness she tastes all the savors of all things with a sure sort of excellence. And without this purgation, in no way whatsoever can she feel and taste the satisfaction of this surpassing abundance of spiritual savors. For if she clings to one single affection even, or any particular thing (habit) whereto the spirit cleaves occasionally or habitually, it is enough to debar her from feeling, tasting, or receiving the exquisite delicacy and intimate savor of the spirit of love, which in itself most preeminently contains all savors.

For, like as the sons of Israel, merely because they still clung to one single affection and memory of the flesh meats they had relished in Egypt, could not enjoy the delicate bread of angels in the desert, which was the Manà, the which as Divine Scripture says, possessed the suavity of all savors, and was converted into that taste which each one loved; so neither can the spirit which still conserves the taint of some occasional or habitual affection or specific knowledge, or any other limited conception, draw nigh to taste the delights of the spirit of liberty in that degree the Will desires. The reason of this is, because the affections, emotions, and conceptions of the perfect spirit, inasmuch as they are so noble and most particularly Divine, are of another sort and kind so different from the physical, that, in order to possess the former immediately and habitually, the latter must be destroyed. Thus it is above all things imperative and necessary, if the soul is to scale these heights of glory, that her baseness be destroyed and dissolved in this dark night of contemplation, she being set into the dark abyss, parched, alone, and empty; because the light that is to be given to her, is a Divine light of the utmost sublimity which transcends all natural light, and cannot be naturally compassed by the mind. And therefore, if the mind is to be enabled to draw nigh to unite itself with this light, and make itself Divine in the state of perfection, it must first be purged and its physical light destroyed, by being, for the time, plunged in darkness by means of this obscure contemplation. In the which darkness it must dwell for so long as shall be necessary to destroy the habit which it has formed and clung to for so long in its mode of understanding, and its place be filled by the Divine Illumination and light. And so, inasmuch as the strength of understanding it possessed before is natural; hence it follows that the darkness it suffers in this night is profound and horrible, and most grievous, since it is felt and touched in the uttermost depths of the spirit. In precisely the same way forasmuch as the love longing which is to be given her in the Divine Union is Divine, and for that reason extremely spiritual, subtle, fine, and delicate, and most intimately interior, since it transcends all natural and imperfect affection, tendency, and emotion of the will, and all its desires, must the will, if it is to be enabled to taste this Divine affection and so sublime delight in the union of love, first be purged and annihilated in all its affections and emotions, and be left parched and anguished, so long as it retains the slightest trace of the natural tendencies whereto it has become habituated, not only in respect of the Divine but of the human. So that, by being extenuated, withered up, and delivered in the fire of this obscure contemplation, from the domination of all its physical thoughts and desires it acquires (like the heart of the fish set by Tobias on the burning embers) a pure and simple disposition, and the palate is purged and made whole in order to feel the sublime and marvelous touches of the Divine love, wherein she shall see herself Divinely transformed, all occasional and habitual oppositions she felt before, being finally expelled. Moreover, as the soul, if she is to enter into the Divine Union whereto she is disposed by this dark night, must be filled with and endowed with a certain glorious magnificence in her intercourse with God, which enshrines innumerable treasures and delights which exceed the utmost abundance that the soul is naturally able to possess (for as Isaiah and St. Paul say: *Oculus non vidit, nec auris audivit, nec in cor hominis ascendit, quæ preparavit Deus iis qui diligunt eum.*[36] Neither eye hath seen, nor ear heard, nor heart conceived what God hath prepared for those who love Him); the soul must be first placed in emptiness and poverty of spirit, by being purged of all support, comfort, and natural conception as to all things above and below, so that she, being thus empty, may be poor of spirit, and stripped of the old Adam, in order to live this new and blessed life whereto she attains by means of this dark night, which is the state of union with God.

And forasmuch as the soul is, at last, destined to acquire a surpassingly noble and delightful sense and perception of all things Divine and human, which doth not fall within her ordinary sensations and knowledge (because she regards them with eyes as different from that they were before, as is the difference between the light and grace of the Holy Ghost and the senses, and the Divine and the human), the spirit must become etherealized and hardened as to the ordinary and bodily sensations; and so, by means of this purgative contemplation, it is placed in intense anguish and conflict, and every friendly and pleasant impression banished from the memory with a most profound sensation and interior conviction of having traveled far away from, and become a stranger to, all things, wherein it seems to her that all are foreign to her and changed from what they were. Because this is the way this night continues to withdraw the spirit from its usual and ordinary and wonted sentiment of things, in order to bring it to the Divine sense, the which is remote and alien from all human ways, so much so, indeed, that it seems to the soul she is beside herself and wandering far away in unknown regions. At others she wonders whether she be not under the spell of some enchantment, or dazzlement; and she goes about rapt in astonishment at the things she sees and hears, which seem to her most wonderful and strange, although they are the same whereof she was frequently wont to discourse. The reason being that the soul is already becoming aloof and alien to her usual senses and ideas respecting things, to the end that, she being deadened to them, may be instructed in those Divine, which belong more to the other life than this. All these afflicting purgations of the spirit the soul suffers, in order that she may be regenerated in the life of the spirit by means of this Divine influence, and through these dolorous pains, at last, give birth to the spirit of Salvation, so that the sentence of Isaiah may be fulfilled which says:

Sic facti sumus à facie tua, Domine. Concepimus, et quasi parturivimus, et peperimus spiritum. From Thy face, O Lord, we conceived, and were as one with pains of travail, and we gave birth to the spirit of Healing. Besides this, since by means of this contemplative night, the soul is disposed to arrive at interior tranquillity and peace, which is of such a nature and so delightful that, as the Scripture says, it exceeds all sense: it is necessary for her that all her former peace (the which, as it was swathed in so many imperfections, was not peace, although seeing that she proceeded to her taste she thought it was peace, peace twice told that is, of the sense and of the spirit) be first purged, and she herself delivered from, and plunged into tribulation on account of this imperfect peace: like as Jeremiah felt and wept for in that text of his we quoted, of set purpose, to set forth the trials of this past night, saying: *Repulsa est à pace anima mea.*[37] My soul is delivered and repelled from peace. This is a grievous confusion of many fears, imaginings and conflicts which the soul wages within herself, wherein her perception of, and grief for, the wretchedness in which she sees herself, brings her to suspect that she is lost, and her favors forever ended. Hence it is that so profound a dolor and groaning entered into the spirit that it makes it burst forth into deep groans and spiritual clamors, sometimes giving vent to loud cries and dissolving into tears when there is strength and virtue to do so; although this relief comes but seldom. The Royal Prophet David has expressed this marvelous well, as one who had, in such good sooth, experienced it, in one of his Psalms saying: *Afflictus sum, et humiliatus sum nimis: rugiebam à gemitu cordis mei.*[38] I was deeply afflicted and humiliated, I roared with the groan of my heart. The which roaring is a most dolorous thing; because, sometimes, with the sudden and acute recollection of her own wretchedness, the soul feels such dolor and grief, that I know not how it may be expressed, save by the simile that Holy Job, when he was in the same conflict, sets forth in the following words: *Tamquam inundantes aquæ sic rugitus meus.* Like as the rushing forth of great waters, so is my bellowing. For like as rivers in full flood submerge and overflow all before them, so doth this roaring and the pangs of the soul wax so great that, inundated and utterly overwhelmed, she is filled with unspeakable anguish and dolor. Such is the operation worked on her by this night, which hides from her all hope of dawn. For, as Job again says concerning this: *Nocte os meum perforatur doloribus: et qui me comedunt, non dormiunt.*[39] By night is my mouth pierced with grief, and they who devor me sleep not. By the mouth is here meant the will, the which is pierced by these pains which neither slumber nor sleep in their laceration of the soul, because the doubts and dreads which so transfix her never cease.

Profound and vast is this battle and combat, since the peace that awaits her shall be most deep; and spiritual grief is internal and rarified and searching, because the love she shall in time possess, must also be most internal and searching. For, inasmuch as the work is to be the more elaborate and exquisite, so much the more exquisite, elaborate and skillful must be the workmanship, and so must the foundation be more deeply laid, the longer the building is to last. Wherefore, as Job says, the soul is withered within herself, and her bowels waxed clamorous without any hope: *Nunc autem in memetipso marscescit anima mea, et possident me dies afflictionis.*[40] So in precisely the same way, when the soul is destined to possess and rejoice in the state of perfection (whereto she journeys by means of this purgative night), in innumerable graces of gifts and virtues (as well in respect of the essence of the soul as of her faculties), so must she first see and feel herself an alien to, and bereft of them all; and be convinced that she is at such a distance from them, that she shall never persuade herself that she will end by attaining them, but that all good, for her, is at an end. As Jeremiah, also, gives us to understand in the same text, when he says: *Oblitus sum bonorum.*[41] I am forgotten of good.

But now let us see why, as this light of contemplation is so soft and pleasant to the soul, as to fulfil all her desires (for, as hath been shewn above, it is the same light wherewith the soul must be finally united and find therein all treasures in the state of perfection she hath longed for), it causeth her, when it first seizeth upon her, these grievous beginnings and searching effects we have here described. It is a question easily to be answered, by repeating what has, already, partly been said, and it is, that the cause thereof is, that although there is nothing in Contemplation and Divine Infusion, which, of itself, can give her pain (rather great suavity and delight, which shall, afterwards, be given to her), yet the weakness and imperfection which still clings to her, and her own inherent tendencies so opposed thereto, prevent her from receiving this suavity and sweetness. And therefore, she is seized upon and enveloped by the Divine light, it causes her to suffer in the way we have described.

WHEREIN THIS PURGATION IS RADICALLY EXPLAINED BY A COMPARISON

For the greater clearness of what has gone before and of what still remains to be said, it must now be noted that this purgative and loving knowledge or Divine Light we speak of, acts on the soul, by purging and preparing her in order to unite her perfectly with itself, in the same way as doth fire on wood, so as to transform it into itself; for the first act of material fire, on reaching the wood, is to dry it, forcing the damp outwards, and making the inward moisture to fall forth in drops. Then it proceeds to blacken, discolor, and disfigure it, until having gradually dried and seasoned it, it makes it glow with light, and expels from it all those ugly and obscure properties which at first opposed the action of the fire. And finally, as the fire gradually kindles the outer parts, and fills them with its heat, it ends at last by transmuting it into itself and transfiguring it into its own essential beauty. The which being done, all action or energy proper to the wood itself ceases (leaving only the bulk and weight thereof less ethereal than that of fire), since it now possesses of itself the properties and motions of fire, for after being thoroughly dried, it becomes heated; and being heated, it gives forth heat; it is lucid and sheds out light; its weight is much less than before, the fire having accomplished in it these properties and effects. After this fashion, then, must we philosophise concerning this Divine fire of love of contemplation, which, before it joins and transforms the soul into itself, first purges her of all her opposite accidents. It drives out her deformities, so that she seems worse than before. For as this Divine purge continues to remove all evil and vicious humors, which by reason of their being so rooted and fixed in the soul, she failed to perceive, and so knew not that so much evil existed within her; so now, in order that they may be cast forth and utterly consumed they are set before her eyes and she sees them so clearly in the illumination of this obscure light of Divine contemplation (although she is no worse than before, either as regards herself or God), that as she perceives within herself what before she saw not, it seems to her that she is such, that not only is she not fit for God to look upon her, but that He must hold her in loathing, and that at last He hates her. By this comparison we may now understand many things in respect of what we now state and are about to state.

In the first place, we are able to understand how and in what manner the same light and loving wisdom which shall finally unite and transform the soul into itself, is the same which, in the beginning, purges and prepares her; like as the fire, which transforms the wood into itself, by becoming a bodily part of it, is one and the same with that which first prepared and seasoned it to receive the action.

In the second place, we shall see, why the soul does not look upon these sufferings as proceeding from the Divine Wisdom, for as says the Wise Man: *Venerunt autem mihi omnia bona pariter cum illas.*[42] All benefits together came to the soul therein; but from her own inherent weakness and imperfection which, without this purgation, did not admit of her receiving this Divine Light, softness and delight (like as the wood which cannot be transformed immediately the fire is put thereto, but must first be prepared and seasoned), and therefore she undergoes great suffering. The which also the Preacher approves, setting forth the sufferings he underwent to the end that he might, at last, be united with, and enjoy this Light, in the following words: *Venter meus conturbatus est quærendo illam: propterea bonam possidebo possessionem.*[43] My soul anguished therein, and my bowels were discomfited in the acquiring it, therefore I shall possess a glad possession.

In the third place, we may hence deduce, in passing, the kind of torture suffered by those in purgatory. For fire would be powerless against them, if they were absolutely fit to reign and be united with God in glory, and had no sins to punish, which is the matter whereon the fire there seizes, the which being consumed, there is nothing left to burn. Likewise here, when once the imperfections have been consumed, the sufferings of the soul are ended, leaving her to rejoice in such sort as this mortal life admits of.

In the fourth place, we shall hence deduce how the soul in the like measure as she is gradually purged and purified by means of this fire of love, becomes more and more inflamed therein; just as the seasoning and preparation of the wood keeps pace with the increase of the heat. Although this kindling of love is not always perceptible to the soul, save at those times when contemplation fails to seize upon her so forcibly, for, then the soul has space to see and, even, to rejoice in the work which is being performed, because the purpose of her sufferings is revealed to her, and they seem to pause a moment from their task, and withdraw the red-hot iron from the furnace, as if to shew the progress they have come to in their labors, and then the soul has time and opportunity to see her own improvement, which she saw not when the work was still going on. So, likewise, when the flame ceases to lick the wood, it affords a chance of observing how far the fire hath spread.

In the fifth place, we shall also deduce from this comparison what has above been said, to wit, how true it is that after these intermissions the soul is replunged into suffering still more intense and exquisitely painful than before. For after she has re-received this proof, and when, at last, the more exterior imperfections have been purified, the fire of love once more seizes upon that which still remains to purify, and consumes it to the heart. Wherein the suffering of the soul is so much the more searching, subtle, and spiritual the more it proceeds to refine and penetrate those imperfections which are most elusive, rarefied, and spiritual; and most firmly rooted in the innermost part. And this happens after the same fashion as with the wood, when the fire, as it makes its way to the interior parts thereof, proceeds with greater force and fury so as to season it to the heart and take absolute possession.

In the sixth place, we shall deduce that, although the soul enjoys great and intensely eager delight in these intervals to such a degree, that, as we said, she thinks at times, that her trials shall never return (although it is most certain that they shall return most quickly), yet she feels, if she is in anyway observant (and at times it forces itself upon her attention), that some fibrous root is left which hinders her from feeling this delight in all its bounty; for it seems as if it threatened to seize upon her once more, and when this is so, it soon returns. In short, that which still remains to be purged and illuminated more interiorly, cannot well be hidden from the soul on account of the purification she has already undergone; like also as in the wood, the difference between the innermost part which still remains to be enlightened, and that which has been already purged is exceedingly apparent; and when this purification again proceeds to attack the more secret parts, one cannot marvel that the soul should think once more that all her mercies have come to an end, and that she dare no longer hope to recover her treasures, since, plunged in more interior emotions, all the more outward good effects are hidden from her. Bearing, then, this comparison in sight together with the explanation already given of the first line of the first song of this dark night and its terrible properties, it will be well to bid farewell to these sad matters of the soul, and now begin to treat of the fruit of her tears and of their happy qualities, whereof the soul begins to sing from this second line.

WHEREIN IS BEGUN TO BE EXPLAINED THE SECOND LINE OF THE FIRST SONG.
IT STATES HOW THE SOUL, AS THE FRUIT OF THESE RIGOROUS CONFLICTS,
FINDS HERSELF WITH A VEHEMENT LONGING AFTER LOVE DIVINE

WITH HEART ACHE KINDLED INTO LOVE

In this line the soul gives us to understand the fire of love that we have spoken of, which after the fashion of the material fire on the wood, proceeds to enflame and kindle her in this night of contemplation. The which kindling, although it is in a certain way like unto that we have above set forth, which took place in the sensitive part of the soul, is, in some manner, as different from this she now speaks of as is the soul from the body or the spiritual part from the sensitive. Because this is a kindling of love in the spirit,[44] wherein, in the midst of these obscure conflicts, the soul feels herself sharply and acutely wounded by a powerful and irresistible Divine love, together with a certain feeling and indistinct presage of God, apart from any specific knowledge or indication; for, as we say, the mind is in darkness.

In this state the impassioned spirit feels the most ardent longings of love; because this spiritual kindling transforms love into passion. For inasmuch as this love is infused in a special way, the soul concurs in it with greater passivity, and so it engenders in her a strong emotion of love. And this love, at length, begins to contain somewhat of the most perfect union with God; and so shares to a certain extent in its properties, the which are more especially acts of God rather than received by the soul herself in her interior, whereto she gives her absolute and amorous consent. But it is the love of God alone which is in process of being united with her, which makes adhere to her this heat and force, temper and passion of love or blazing forth as the soul now calls it. The which love finds so much the more room and disposition in the soul to unite with, and to wound her, the more it hath shut, alienated, and incapacitated all her appetites from the power to take delight in anything of Heaven or earth. The which in this dark purgation, as has been said, happens on a large scale, since God has so weaned and gathered together the powers, that they may not relish anything they were fain to. All which God does to the end that, as He hath withdrawn and gathered them all together for Himself, the soul may have greater strength and capacity to receive this strong Union of Love of God, which through this purgative remedy, He, at length, begins to give her, wherein she is called upon to love with all her strength and sensitive desires; the which could not be if they were scattered abroad in the search of some other enjoyment. Wherefore so that David might be enabled to receive the force of love in this Union of God, He said to him: *Fortitudinem meam ad te custodiam.*[45] My strength I will keep for thee: that is, the entire capacity and desires and strength of my powers, having no will to employ their activity or taste in any other thing save Thee.

From this, we may, after some fashion, estimate how strong and fierce must this kindling of love in the spirit be, where God holds gathered in all the forces, powers, and desires of the soul, spiritual as well as sensitive, so that, blending into one harmonious whole, they employ all their virtue and vitality on this love, that so the first precept may be complied with, in very truth and in the utmost perfection, which, not rejecting from this love anything of man nor excluding anything he hath, says: Thou shalt love thy God with all thy heart, with all thy mind, with all thy soul, and with all thy strength. *Diliges Dominum Deum tuum ex toto corde tuo, et tota anima tua, et ex tota fortitudine tua.*[46]

All the appetites and powers of the soul, being now folded inwards in this bursting forth of love, the soul having been wounded and chastened in regard to all of them, and aflame with love; what may we understand shall be the motions and tendencies of all these powers and appetites, when they see themselves ablaze and wounded with overpowering and unsatisfied love, in darkness and doubt thereof, surely suffering a keener hunger as their experience of God enlarges? For the touch of this love and fire Divine dries up the spirit in such a fashion and sets light to the longings that consume to such a degree that, to quench its thirst, it wanders restlessly to and fro, and longs for God after a thousand ways and manners, with that greed and fierce desire which David in his Psalm so well sets forth saying: *Sitivit in te anima mea: quàm multipliciter tibi caro mea.*[47] My soul thirsted for Thee: how often after many ways doth my flesh ache after Thee: that is, in desire. And another translation saith: My soul thirsted for Thee, my soul perisheth because of Thee.

This is the reason why the soul says in the verse: "With heart ache kindled into love." Because in all her affairs and thoughts that she revolves within herself, and in all the businesses and matters put before her, she loves in many ways, and desires and languishes with desire after the same fashion as did David in many ways, in all times and places, able to find rest in nothing, tormented by this burning longing and mortal wound, like as St. Job gives us to understand, saying: *Sicut cervus desiderat umbram, et sicut mercenarius præstolatur finem operis sui: sic et ego habui menses vacuos, et noctes laboriosas enumeravi mihi. Si dormiero, dicam quando consurgam? Et rursum extectabo vesperam, et replebor doloribus usque ad tenebras.*[48] Like as the hart desireth the shade, and the hireling the end of his labor, so were the months void to me, and I counted the weary and laborious nights. If I lay me down to sleep I shall say: When shall I rise? And immediately I shall hope for the evening, and I shall be full of grief until the night fall. For such a soul everything on earth becomes all too narrow, she cannot contain herself, neither earth nor Heaven itself can hold her, and she is full of woe until the night fall that

Job here speaks of, which, to speak spiritually and to our purpose, is a suffering and torture unmitigated by any certain hope of spiritual light and favor. Whence her longing and woe in this furnace of love wax greater, inasmuch as it is multiplied twice over. First by the spiritual darkness wherein she sees herself, which afflicts her with its doubts and fears. Second by the love of God which inflames and stings her with its amorous wounding, and most marvelously incites her. The which two sorts of suffering in a like season Isaiah sets forth exceeding well, in the words: *Anima mea desideravit te in nocte.*[49] My soul desired Thee in the nighttime, that is, in wretchedness. And this is one of the ways of suffering caused by this dark night; but with my spirit, saith he, in my bowels until the morning will I watch for thee: *Sed et spiritu meo in præcordüs meis de mane vigilabo ad te.*[50]

And this is the second way of suffering in the desire and longing caused by the love in the bowels of the spirit, which are the spiritual affections. But in the midst of these obscure and amorous pains the soul feels a certain inward presence and power, which abides with, and fills her with such strength, that if this weight of dense and heavy darkness vanishes, she ofttimes feels void, forlorn, and weak. And the cause is that, then, like as the force and activity of the soul was inspired and instilled by the dark fire of love which enveloped her, she being passive; thence it is, that when it ceases to envelop her, the darkness ceases, as also the heat and force of love within her.

SHEWS HOW THIS TERRIBLE NIGHT IS PURGATORY, AND HOW THEREIN THE
DIVINE WISDOM ILLUMINATES MEN ON EARTH WITH THE SAME ILLUMINATION
WHICH PURGES AND ILLUMINATES THE ANGELS IN HEAVEN

From what has been already said we shall see how this obscure night of loving fire, like as its purging operations are effected in darkness, so also in darkness is the soul gradually set afire. We shall also see, that, just as the predestined are purged in the other life with dark and material fire; they are purged and cleansed in this life with loving, dark, and spiritual fire. For this is the difference, that there, they are cleansed by fire, and here they are cleansed and illuminated by love. The which love David craved, when he said: *Cor mundum crea in me,*

Deus, etc.[51] For cleanness of heart is not less important than the love and grace of God. For the pure of heart are called by our Savior Blessèd; the which is as if He had called them lovers, for blessedness is given for nothing less than love.

And that the soul is purged in the illumination of this fire of loving wisdom (for God never gives mystical wisdom without love, since love itself infuses it) Jeremiah well shews, saying: *De excelso misit ignem in ossibus meis, et erudivit me.*[52] He sent fire into my bones, and taught me. And David says that the Wisdom of God is silver proved in the purgative fire of love: *Eloquia Domini, eloquia casta; argentum igne examinatum.*[53] For this obscure contemplation inspires in the soul love and wisdom conjointly, to each one according to his need and capacity, enlightening the soul and purging her of her ignorance, as says the Wise One, that so it wrought with him: *Ignorantias meas illuminavit.*[54]

Hence we likewise infer that these souls are purged and illuminated by the very same Wisdom of God which purges the angels of their blindness, emanating from God through the highest Hierarchies to the lowest, and thence to men. For which reason all the works done by angels and their inspirations, are said with truth and propriety in the Scriptures to be done not only by God but by them; for, as a rule, they emanate from Him through them, and are flashed from one to the other without pause or stay: like as a sunbeam when it strikes on many windows placed in a certain relative order, is flashed from one to the other. For although it is true that of itself the ray strikes upon all; still, each one transmits and infuses it into the next in a more modified form, with more or less sharpness and brilliancy, conformably to the position of the window, just as it happens to be farther off or nearer the Sun. Whence it follows, that the higher and inferior spirits, inasmuch as they are closer to God, are more thoroughly purged and clarified with a more drastic purgation; and that those who come last will receive this illustration after a more attenuated and distant fashion. Whence it follows, that, since man is inferior to the angels, when God wills to give him this contemplation he is obliged to receive it after his more limited fashion and with pain and suffering. Because the light of God which illuminates the angel, making him shine with splendor, and flame resplendently with love, he being a pure spirit disposed for such an infusion, man on account of his impurity and weakness, it, as a rule, illuminates (as has been said above) in darkness, suffering and conflict (like the Sun which shining on a weak eye, causes it pain and anguish), until this same fire of love shall have spiritualized and etherealized him, by its purificative influence, and enables him to receive this amorous influx with entire serenity after the fashion of the angels, he being now purged, as with the Lord's assistance we shall presently set forth; for souls there are which even in this life have received more perfect illumination than the angels. But in the meanwhile, he receives this contemplation and loving impression in the conflict and passionate longing we have said. Not always, however, doth the soul continue to feel this blazing forth and passionate love and longing. For, when this spiritual purgation at first begins, the entire strength of this Divine fire is chiefly directed towards drying up and seasoning the timber of the soul, rather than in giving her heat; but when at last this fire begins to burn within the soul, very often doth she feel this flame and heat of love. Now as the intellect becomes increasingly purged by means of this darkness, it sometimes happens that this mystical and amorous theology besides inflaming the will, likewise wounds the neighboring power of intellect, enlightening it with a certain Divine cognition and luster so sweetly and divinely, that the will, by its assistance, becomes marvelously fervent, this Divine fire of Love blazing up within her in flames of living light, after such a fashion that now with the lively knowledge which is given her, it appears to the soul a living fire. And it is of this state that David speaks in one of his Psalms: *Concaluit cor meum intra me: et in meditatione mea exardescet ignis.*[55] My heart waxed hot within me, and the flame was so intense, that I thought it was on fire. And this glow of love with the union of these two powers, the intellect and the will, is, for the soul, a priceless and delicious thing. For it is certain that in this obscurity, she has already attained the beginnings of the perfection of the union of love she hopes for. And, therefore, doth she not arrive at this touch of so sublime a sense and love of God, unless she has previously gone through many trials, and a large share of the purgation. But for other and lower grades which are more generally met with, so great a purgation is not needed.

OF OTHER SOOTHING AND TENDER EFFECTS EFFECTED ON THE SOUL BY THIS OBSCURE NIGHT OF CONTEMPLATION

After this fashion of a flaming fire we may understand certain of the soothing effects which this obscure night of contemplation now proceeds to work upon the soul; for sometimes, in the midst of this darkness, the soul is enlightened, and the light shines forth upon the darkness, this mystic influence descending full upon the intellect, and the will sharing therein to some degree, with a serenity and purity so rare and delightful to the sense of the soul, that it is impossible to define it, sometimes in one way of feeling God, at others in another. Sometimes, likewise, conjointly with the other powers, it transfixes the will, and sets it on fire with a sublime, tender and powerful love; for we have already said that, sometimes, these two powers, the intellect and the will are united, and the more completely the intellect is purged, so much the more perfect and delicate are its perceptions. But before attaining to this state, it is more usual for this kindling spark to touch the will than for the spark of perfect knowledge to touch the intellect.

This glow and thirst of love, as it now, at length, proceeds from the Holy Spirit, is absolutely different from that we described in the night of the sense. For although in this the senses also have their share, since they fail not to participate in the conflict of the spirit, still the root and the sting of the thirst of love is felt in the higher part of the soul, that is, in the Spirit, which feels and grasps its sensations and the lack of what it most desires, after such a fashion, that all the tortures of the senses, although, without comparison, greater than in the first sensitive night, it counts as nothing, because it apprehends in its most secret depths the want of a great gift, and a void that nothing else can fill.

But here it must be noted that, although at first, when this spiritual night commences, this flame of love is not felt, owing to this fire of love not having begun to work, still, in its place, God from the first bestows upon the soul so great an instinctive love of Him that, as we have said, her chief suffering and grief in the trials of this night is the terror that haunts her that God is lost to her and that she is forsaken of Him. And so we can, with reason, assert that, from the beginning of this night the soul is constantly wounded with longing for love, before instinctive, now, also, inflammatory. And it is seen that the greatest distress she feels amidst her trials is this dread; for if she could then be sure that she is not entirely lost or doomed, but that what she passes through is for the best (as indeed it is), and that God is not angry, all her sufferings would not cost her a single thought, rather would she rejoice, knowing that it is God's goodwill and pleasure. For so great is the instinctive love she feels for God, even when it is shrouded from her in darkness, that, not only would she do this but rejoice greatly to die a thousand deaths to serve Him. But when, at length, the flame has kindled in her, conjointly with the instinctive love she already bears to God, she achieves such energy and vigor, and so great a longing after God, communicated to her by the heat of love, that greatly daring, without regarding aught, nor having respect to any mortal thing, in the strength and intoxication of her passion, without much heeding what she does, she would perform whatsoever strange and unwonted things were presented to her, no matter by what mode or fashion, so long as it brings her to Him who loves her.

This is the cause why Mary Magdalene, in spite of her noble rank, held the crowd of great and lesser men gathered together at the banquet made in the Pharisee's house of no account, as saith St. Luke, and stayed not to consider that it was out of place and looked unseemly to go and weep and shed tears amidst the guests, so long as she (without an hour's delay, waiting for another time and season) might come into His presence for whom her very soul was wounded and inflamed. And this is the intoxication and daring of love, that although she knew that her Belovèd was shut up in the sepulchre sealed with a great stone and surrounded by a guard of soldiers, none of these things could stop her from setting forth before the dawn with the nard and ointments to anoint Him. And finally, this, her intoxication and passionate love made her ask of him whom she took to be the gardener and believed to have robbed Him from the tomb, to tell her, if so be he had taken the body, where he had laid it, so that she might take possession of it: *Situ sustulisti eum, dicito mihi ubi posuisti eum, et ego eum tollam,*[56] not considering as she would have done, if her judgment and reason had been free and unbiased, that such a question was far from prudent, since it is clear that had he robbed the body, he would not certainly own it, and far less allow her to take it from him; for the vehemence and passion of love possesses this property, that it thinks all things possible, and that everyone is seeking what it seeks itself; nor can it believe that any other person can be busied and eager about aught else, save that, itself seeks and loves. And for this reason when the Bride went forth to seek her lover in the squares and outskirts of the city, thinking that everyone she met were bent on the same errand, she said to them, that if they found him, they were to tell him from her that she was suffering for his love. Such, then, was the love of this Mary, that she thought that if the gardener would only tell her where he had hidden the body, she would go thither and take it (whosoever might bid her nay). Of this stature, then, are the agonies of love this soul begins to feel, when she has, at length, come so far upon her journey through this spiritual purgation. For she rises up by night (that is, in this purgative night) in answer to the impulses of her will. And with the agony and strength that the lioness or the bear goes forth to seek her cubs when she has been robbed of them and cannot find them, so doth this wounded soul go out to seek her God. For, as she is in darkness, she feels herself without Him, and dies for love of Him. And this is the restless love wherein a living person cannot long exist unless he receives some return or dies, like unto the longing which Rachel had for children when she said to Jacob: *Da mihi liberos, alioquin moriar.*[57] Give me children: if not, I die.

But it is here to be observed, how it is that the soul, feeling herself in such misery and so unworthy of God, as she does in this purgative darkness, yet possesses such daring and intrepid strength as to go forth to join Him. The reason is, that as love now begins to give her strength so that she loves in very sooth, and the property of love is to tend to unite with, join, bring down to its own level, and assimilate with itself the thing loved to *the end that it may* be perfected in the gifts of love; hence it is, that this soul not being perfected in love since she has not yet attained to union, the hunger and thirst that beset her for that she lacks, which is union, and the strength that love has now infused into the will, filling it with passionate desire, makes her bold and intrepid as regards the ardent will, although, the mind being still in darkness, she feels herself unworthy and miserable.

Nor will I omit to set down here the reason why, since this Divine Light is always light for the soul, it does not as soon as it falls upon her, fill her with its radiance, as it afterwards does, but rather produces the darkness and woe we have described. Somewhat has been already said, but to this particular question it is answered: that the darkness and the other ills which the soul experiences when this Divine Light assaults, are not darkness nor ills on the part of the light itself, but on that of the soul, and the light enlightens her, so that she may see them. Whence this Divine Light shines upon her from the first; but the soul cannot at once see thereby, that which is closest to her, or to be more exact, within her, which is her darkness or wretchedness which she, at length, discerns through the mercy of God, whereas before, she saw them not, because this supernatural light shone not upon her. And this is the reason why, at first, she feels only darkness and the sense of her own wickedness.

But directly she has been purged by the knowledge of, and sorrow for, her sins, her eyes shall be opened and display to her the graces of this light Divine; and all these shadows and imperfections of the soul being expelled and removed, the great benefits and mercies she hath gradually reaped in this blessed night, shall at length come into view, so that, by slow degrees, she shall know and recognize them.

From what has been said, it is evident why it is that God showers mercies on the soul by cleansing her with this strong lye and bitter purge, as regards the sensitive and spiritual part from all the affections and imperfect habits inherent to her as to things temporal and physical, sensitive and spiritual, by clouding over her interior faculties, and voiding and emptying them of all these things, and constraining and withering up her sensitive and spiritual inclinations, and weakening and lessening the natural strength of the soul in respect to them (the which the soul, by her own efforts alone, could never have achieved as we shall presently tell), this being the method whereby God deprives her of strength for all that is not God, so that He may gradually clothe her anew, after the old skin has been, at length, peeled and stripped off. And thus, like the eagle, she renews her youth, and remains clad with the new man, created, as saith the Apostle, after the image of God: *Et induite novum hominem, qui secundum Deum creatus est.*[58] The which is nothing else than the enlightening of the intellect with supernatural light, so that the human mind be made Divine united with the Divine. And, in precisely the same way, doth He inflame the will with Divine love, after such sort that the will, at length, is not less than Divine, loving no less than divinely, welded and united in one with the Divine will and love; and the memory the same, and the inclinations and appetites all likewise changed to the image of God, divinely. And thus this soul shall, at length, be a heavenly soul, celestial, and more Divine than human. All which, as will have been clearly evident by what we have said, God gradually works and performs in the soul by means of this night, shedding His light upon her and making her flame up divinely with longings for Him alone, and for no other thing besides. Wherefore, most justly and reasonably, the soul then adds the third line of the song, which, together with the remainder thereof, we shall set down and explain in the following chapter.

WHEREIN IS SET DOWN AND EXPLAINED THE THREE LAST LINES OF THE FIRST
SONG

> Oh blessed chance!
> I stole me forth unseen,
> My house being wrapt in sleep.

The blissful chance chanted by the soul in the first of these three lines, was effected by that she sings of in the two next lines, where she uses the metaphor of one who, the better to carry out his purpose, sets forth from his house at night and under shadow of darkness, the inmates of the house being now at rest, so that none shall hinder his departure. For as this soul was bent on sallying forth to accomplish a Deed so rare and heroic, which was the uniting of herself with her Divine Lover, she goes forth abroad, since the Lover is only to be found without in solitude. Wherefore the Bride desired to find him unaccompanied, saying: *Quis mihi det te fratrem meum sugentem ubera matris meæ, ut inveniamte foris, et deosculer te.*[59] Who shall give thee to me, oh! My brother! That I may find thee abroad, and share my love with thee? So likewise was the passionate soul compelled, if she would achieve her desired end, to do the same also, and to go forth by night, when all the servants of her house are sleeping and at rest; that is, the inferior operations, emotions, and appetites of her soul extinguished and put to sleep by means of this night, which are the inmates of the house who, ever on the watch, allure the soul from these her treasures, averse to her wresting from them her liberty. For these are the servants whereof our Savior speaks in the sacred Gospel, who are the enemies of man: *Et inimici hominis domestici ejus.*[60] And so it was essential that their labors and movements should be laid to sleep in this night, to the end that they hold not back the soul from the supernatural gifts of the union of love of God, which cannot be achieved so long as they are astir with vitality and movement. For all action and movement on their part do rather hinder than assist in the receiving of the spiritual wealth of the union of love. For, inasmuch as all natural capacity is inadequate in respect of the supernatural favors which God, by His infusion alone, inspires in the soul passively, secretly, and in silence. And so, in order to receive it, it is necessary that all the faculties be laid under this spell of silence, so that they shall not obtrude thereon their inferior activity and vile inclinations.

But it was for this soul a blissful chance that God, in this night, holds all the inmates of her house in sleep; that is, all the faculties, emotions, affections and appetites which dwell in the spiritual soul, to the end that she may arrive at the spiritual union of perfect love of God "with none to note"; to wit, without being hindered of them, forasmuch as she has left them wrapped in slumber and mortified in this night, as has been said. Oh, how fortunate a chance it is for the soul to be able to free herself from the abode of her sensuality.

None, indeed, can understand it, to my thinking, save the soul which has tasted thereof. For she will clearly see how miserable was the servitude which bound her, and how great the number of the wretched trifles which enslaved her when she was in bondage to the savory taste of her appetites and passions, and she shall know how that the life of the Spirit is true liberty and riches, which bring with them inestimable mercies. Whereof we shall proceed to set down some in the following songs, wherein it shall be more clearly seen how right the soul is to look upon the passage of this dolorous and awesome night as a most glorious and blessed chance.

WHICH GIVES THE SECOND SONG AND ITS EXPOSITION

> Into the darkness, and yet safe,
> By secret stair and in disguise,
> Oh gladsome hap!
> In darkness, and in secret I crept forth,
> My house being wrapt in sleep.

In this Song the soul still proceeds to sing certain properties of the darkness of this night, repeating the good fortune that she derived therefrom. She speaks of them, as if she replied to some certain tacit objection, warning us that we must not think that, because she has passed through such tortures of anguish, doubt, dread and horror in this night and darkness, as has been said, she ran any the more danger of being lost: nay, in the darkness of this night, did she rather find herself; for therein did she free herself and subtly escape from her opponents, who at all times blocked the way, for in the darkness of the night she walked safely, having changed her raiment, and disguised herself under the three liveries or colors we shall presently describe; and by a most secret stair, for no one in the house knew of it (which, as we shall likewise observe in its proper place, is living Faith). She stole forth so disguised and noiselessly, so as to accomplish her great Deed, that she could not but go secure and in the utmost safety; the more especially as the sensitive and intellectual appetites, inclinations, and passions are now asleep, mortified, and extinguished in this purgative night, which, had they been awake and active, would have stopped her journey.

THE FIRST LINE IS SET DOWN AND IT IS SHEWN HOW IT IS THAT THE SOUL
PROCEEDS IN SAFETY, THOUGH HER JOURNEY IS WRAPT IN DARKNESS

We have now seen that the darkness the soul here speaks of, is in respect of the appetites and sensitive faculties, interior and spiritual, whose natural light is completely clouded over in this night, so that being purged therefrom, they may be illumined with the supernatural light; because the sensitive and spiritual appetites are asleep and deadened, powerless to taste the sweetness of anything whatsoever, whether human or Divine: the inclinations of the soul oppressed and chained, unable to act or lean on any stay; the imagination fettered and incapable of any useful thought; the memory annihilated; the mind clouded over; and hence, also, the will parched and suffocated, and all the faculties void and empty, and above all this a dense and heavy cloud suspended over the soul herself, which keeps her in anguish and, as it were, estranged from God. In this way "in the dark," she says, she walked "secure." The reason of this is indeed evident: because, as a rule the soul never errs save through her appetites or tastes, or her thoughts, or her impressions, or her inclinations, wherein as a rule she exceeds or falls short, or varies, or dotes, and thence is bent to evil doing.

Whence it is clear that, since all these operations and activity are now checked, the soul is safe from falling into error. For not only is she delivered from herself, but also from her other enemies which are the world and the devil, which, when the affections and operations of the soul are extinguished, no loophole or weak point is left for them to attack.

Hence it follows that the more utter the darkness which surrounds the soul on her journey, and the more vastated she is of her natural operations, so doth she proceed in greater safety. For, as says the prophet: *Perditio tua Israel: tantummodo in me auxilium tuum*,[61] the perdition of the soul comes solely from herself (that is, from her operations and interior and sensitive appetites at war one with another), and good, saith God, cometh from Me alone. Therefore, she being thus impeded by her own sins, it remains for the gifts of union with God, presently to flow into her appetites and faculties, which shall make them Divine and celestial. Whence, in the season of this darkness, if the soul is intent thereon, she will soon, and in very truth, see how little the appetites and powers are led astray after vain and useless things; and how safe she is from vain glory, and pride and presumption, frivolous and false enjoyment, and from many other things. Then, indeed, it follows that, not only because she walks in darkness, is she not only not lost, but even greatly rescued, since now she is on the way to gain all virtues.

But as to the immediate doubt which this at once gives rise to, to wit, wherefore, since the things of God are of themselves beneficial to the soul, and win her, and secure her (in all goodness), doth He, in this night, cloud over her appetites and faculties in respect of these good things, to such a point that she neither enjoys them nor treats them as she does other things, and even in some sort less? The answer is that it is most essential for her, at this time, to be voided from and deprived of her own activity and inclination in respect, even, of spiritual things. Because her faculties and appetites are still degraded and impure; and so, although were God to give them the taste and perception of spiritual and Divine things, they could not receive them, save most meanly and imperfectly. For, as says the philosopher, the thing received partakes of the nature of the recipient. Whence, since these physical and mental powers have neither strength, purity, nor capacity to receive and taste of supernatural things as they are in themselves, that is Divine, but according to their own limitations; it is likewise necessary to cast them into darkness, and shroud from them these Divine [operations], to ensure a more perfect purgation. To the end that, being first weaned, purged, and their first nature brought to nought, they may lose this base fashion of acting and receiving, and all the powers and appetites of the soul be seasoned, disposed and attuned to receive, perceive, and taste of the Divine after a lofty and sublime manner, the which may not be, unless the old Adam be first destroyed. Hence it is that all things spiritual, if they do not (sent by the Father of Light), descend from above upon the human free will and appetite, they cannot, in spite of all man's efforts to exercise his taste and appetite and faculties on God, and however much it may seem to them that they taste of Him, they do not taste of Him in this other manner; that is, divinely and perfectly. As to which (if this were the place) we might here set forth how many there are who experience many gusts and desires and motions of the faculties in regard to God and spiritual things, and, perchance, account them to be super-natural and spiritual, whereas, they are, probably, nothing more than entirely physical and human acts and desires, which, as they are produced on them by other things as well, proceed from a certain constitutional facility to direct the desires and powers to any object whatever. If, perchance, occasion offers, we shall treat of it later on, and shew by certain signs when the interior motions and actions of the soul are entirely physical, and when entirely spiritual, and when both spiritual and physical in respect of intercourse with God. Suffice it to say here, that if these interior acts and impulses of the soul are to arrive at being moved by God sublimely and divinely, they must first be put to sleep and darkened, and all natural capacity and activity stilled, until they are entirely deprived of strength.

Then, oh! Spiritual Soul, when thou shalt see thy inclination dark-ened, thy affections withered up and crushed, and thy faculties disabled for all interior exercise, let it not grieve thee, rather count it for great good fortune; for God is even now on the way to deliver thee from thyself, taking from thee thy possessions; wherewith, however will-ingly they helped thee, thou couldest not proceed so consummately, perfectly, and safely (because of their impurity and unskillfulness), as now, when God takes thee by the hand and leads thee like a blind man through the darkness, whither and by what paths thou knowest not, nor wouldst ever succeed in reaching, guided by thine own eyes and feet, however well thou mightest travel.

The reason likewise, wherefore the soul not only goes in safety, when she thus sets forth in darkness, but, even, at every step conquers and improves [in good], is that, as a rule, when she continues to receive some fresh grace and gift, it comes from a source the least comprehensible to her, nay, on the contrary, rather doth she think that she is on the road to perdition. Because, as she has never experienced this strange and unwonted thing which dazzles and bewilders her in respect of all her preconceptions and former methods of procedure, rather doth she think that she has lost her way than that she draws nearer to the goal of her achievement, since she sees that she is lost to all she knew and delighted in before and wanders by an unknown and unpleasing road. Just as the traveler, who, to reach strange and foreign lands, travels along unfamiliar and unpracticed roads where all knowledge of his own is useless and he must trust to the guidance of others: for it is clear that he cannot get to foreign lands save by foreign and unfamiliar roads, those he knew being left behind; so in like manner the soul, when she is making the most progress, wanders in darkness and regions to her unknown. Therefore, God, being now, as we have said, the Teacher of this poor blind soul, well may she, when at last she comes forth into light, and perceives the steps whereby she has been led, rejoice with exceeding joy and cry: "In darkness and yet safe."

Another reason, likewise, is there why the soul hath journeyed safely through this darkness, and it is, that she has suffered: for the way of suffering is safer and even more beneficial than that of enjoyment and action. First, because in suffering she acquires strength from God, and in action and enjoyment she exercises her weakness and imperfections. And next, because in suffering she practices and acquires virtue and purifies the soul, and makes her wiser and more cautious. But, now, there is another cause still more potent why she travels in darkness and yet goes safely, and it is on account of the light already spoken of, or the obscure wisdom. For this dark night of contemplation so absorbs and holds her within itself, and sets her so close to God, that it protects and delivers her from all that is not God. For, as the soul is placed in this state so that she may be healed of her infirmities and recover her health, which is God Himself, His Majesty puts her on a diet and abstinence from all things, and turns away her appetite for them; just as a sick man who is beloved by those of his household is guarded by them in such seclusion that they allow not a breath of air to touch him, and shut out the joyous light of day, and go on tiptoe so that he shall not hear their footfalls, and silence all sound and rumor in the house, and give him to eat most delicate food and in careful measured quantities, more nourishing than appetizing.

All these properties (since all are for the safety and protection of the soul) this obscure contemplation produces in her, because she is placed nearer to God. For, in very truth, the closer the soul gets to Him, so, by reason of her weakness, is she plunged in deeper darkness and more profound obscurity; just as one who gazes into the eye of the sun would only find his eyes darkened and injured by its overpowering splendor, by reason of the weakness, impurity, and limitations of his vision.

Hence, it follows that so vast is the spiritual light of God and so greatly doth it transcend the intellect, that the closer it approaches, the more it is blinded and obscured. And this is the reason wherefore David says, that God set the darkness for His hiding place, and the clouds for His covering, and His tabernacle about Him, dark water in the clouds of the air, *Et posuit tenebras latibulum Suum, in circuitu ejus tabernaculum ejus: tenebrosa aqua in nubibus aëris.*[62] The which dark water in the clouds of the air is the obscure contemplation and Divine Wisdom in the soul, as we are saying. The which as God gradually joins them more closely to Himself they feel as something very close to the Tabernacle where He dwells. And thus that which in God is light and a most sublime clarity, is obscure shadow for man (as saith St. Paul) and as the Royal Prophet David declares in the same Psalm, saying, *Præ fulgore in conspectu ejus nubes transierunt.*[63] By reason of the splendor that dwells in his presence, clouds and cataracts went forth (to wit, for the physical intellect) whose light, as saith Isaiah: *Obtenebrata est in caligine ejus.* Oh wretched lot of this our life, where we get to know the truth with so much difficulty! Since the clearest and most radiant [light] and truth itself, is for us most dark and doubtful; and for this reason we fly from it, being that we have most need of; and that which glitters and fills our eyes with luster, we embrace and follow after, being that which is worst for us, and makes us fall at every step. How great is the fear and danger man lives in, since the very physical light of his eyes which leads him, is the first to dazzle and betray him on his journey towards God. So that, if he would clearly perceive the road whereby

he travels, he must, of force, keep his eyes fast shut and go in darkness, so as to be safe from the domestic enemies of his household,
which are his own senses and faculties! Well, then fares it with the
soul when she is hidden and protected in this dark water, which is
close to God. For like as it serves to God Himself, for a tabernacle
and sanctuary, so shall it serve for the same to her, and for an
absolute shelter and place of safety where, in spite of the darkness
she is hidden and sheltered from herself and from all hurt from any
creature, as we have said; because of blessed souls like these it is that
David speaks in another Psalm: *Abscondes los in abscondito faciei tuæ ā*
conturbatione hominum: proteges eos in tabernaculo tuo á contradictione
linguarum.[64] Thou shalt hide them in the secret place of thy counte-
nance from the tumult of men; thou shalt guard them in thy
tabernacle from the strife of tongues, wherein is included all manner
of protection; for to be hidden in the face of God from the turbu-
lence of men, is to be fortified by this obscure contemplation against
every danger that can overtake them on the part of man. And for the
soul to be thus sheltered and bestowed in His sanctuary from the rage
of tongues, is for her to be engulfed in this dark water, which is the
tabernacle of David, as we have said. Whence, since the soul is weaned
from all appetites and affections, and her faculties obscured, she is
free from every imperfection that stands in the way of her spiritual
[progress], whether arising from her own carnality or any other
creature. Therefore this soul may well cry, that she walks "in darkness and in safety."

There is, likewise, another reason of no less efficacy than the
preceding, whereby we may, at length, rest convinced that this soul
is on the right road, although in darkness, and this is the strength
which, from the first, this dark, painful, and gloomy water of God
inspires in her. For in short, although it is overshadowed with gloom,
it is, still, water, and, therefore, shall not fail to regenerate and fortify
the soul in that she has most need of, although in darkness and great
agony. Because, as soon as the soul perceives within herself a sincere
determination and active power to do nothing she knows to be an
offense against God, nor to leave undone that which seems to her to
be for His service. Because this obscure love cleaves to her with an

exceeding vigilant interior care and solicitude as to that she shall do or fail to do for Him to please Him, being ever on the watch ceaselessly tormented as to whether she has given Him cause for anger; and all this with far more eagerness and anxiety than before, as has been above described in the chapter on the longings of love. For now every appetite and force and faculty of the soul, since they are gathered in from all other things, direct their whole exertions and strength towards pleasing their God alone. After this fashion doth the soul go forth from herself and all created things to the sweet and delightful union of love of God, "In darkness, and in safety."

THE SECOND LINE IS SET DOWN AND AN EXPLANATION GIVEN AS TO WHY THIS DARK CONTEMPLATION IS SECRET

BY SECRET STAIR AND IN DISGUISE

It behoves us to set forth three properties in respect of three words contained in the line before us. Two of these, which are "secret" and "stair," belong to the dark night of contemplation we are describing; but the third, which is "disguised," has to do with the conduct of the soul in this night. As to the first, we must know that the soul here in this line calls the obscure contemplation, whereby she sets forth on her journey to the union of love, the "secret stair," by reason of two properties it contains which we shall proceed to state. First she calls this darksome contemplation secret; forasmuch as we have above hinted, it is the mystical theology, which the theologians style SECRET WISDOM, and is, as saith Santo Tomàs, communicated to us and infused into the soul more particularly by love. And this takes place secretly in the darkness of the natural workings of the mind and of the other faculties. Whence, in so far as the said faculties attain not thereto, unless the Holy Spirit infuses it into the soul, which knows not how or whence it comes and is ignorant of its nature, as saith the Bride in the Songs, it is called secret. And, in good sooth, not only doth the Soul not understand it, but no one does, not even the devil himself. Forasmuch as the Master who teaches it dwells substantially within her. And not on this account alone may it be called secret, but also by reason of the effects it works upon the soul. For not only is this

SECRET WISDOM secret when it purges the soul in the darkness and affliction of the purgation because she herself is utterly at a loss as to how to describe it; but, likewise, after she has been illuminated, when this WISDOM is communicated to her more clearly and with greater distinctness, does it remain so hidden from her discernment and capacity to refer to it by any name, that apart from the invincible repugnance the soul feels to speak of it, she finds no way or mode, nor adequate simile, capable of expressing or in anyway shadowing forth a KNOWLEDGE so transcendent and a spiritual sensation so delicate and infused. And so, however desirous she might be to describe it, and in spite of all language she might use, it would ever remain secret and hidden. For as this Inner Wisdom is so absolute, so all embracing and spiritual, that it entered not into the mind cloaked or disguised under any species or image subject to the sense, as sometimes happens; hence it is that the senses and imaginative faculty (when it entered not through them nor bore their vesture and complexion) can give no explanation nor conception thereof that can in anyway enable them to express it, however slightly, although the soul clearly sees that she knows and tastes of this delicate and most marvelous Wisdom.

Like as one who should perceive a thing, the like of which had never been seen before, nor anything the least approaching it, although he might know and take delight therein, would not know what to call it nor how to describe it, for all the efforts he might make, and this in spite of its being distinctly perceptible to the senses; how much less, then, can one make clear what never entered therein? For the speech of God possesses this property: that when it is most secret, infused and spiritual, as to transcend all sense, it instantly suspends and silences the whole harmony and ability of the exterior and interior senses. Whereof we have instances and examples in the Divine Scripture. For the difficulty of setting forth and explaining it outwardly in words, Jeremiah made evident when, after God had spoken with him, he could say nought but a.a.a. And the dulness of the interior, that is, of the inner sense of the imagination conjointly with the exterior sense in respect of this, Moses also made proof of in the presence of God in the burning bush, when he not only said to God, that after he had spoken with Him, he knew not how, nor was able, to speak; but did not even (as it saith in the Acts of the Apostles) dare to behold, as it seemed to him that the imagination was far away and silent: *Tremefactus autem Moises non audebat considerare.*[65] For as the Wisdom of this contemplation is the speech of God to the soul in pure spirit, as the senses are not purely spiritual they behold it not, and so it is hidden from them and they are powerless to know or give it expression.

Whence we may deduce the reason why some certain simple and fearful souls who journey along this road, were fain to describe their experiences to their spiritual guide, and cannot and know not how, and so feel the utmost repugnance to speak thereof; more especially when the contemplation is somewhat finer and more subtle as scarce to be perceived by the soul herself; and they can only describe it by saying that the soul is satisfied and serene or happy, and that they discern the presence of God, and that, to their thinking, all is well with them; but that it is impossible to express what the soul experiences, save in general terms similar to those mentioned. It is another thing altogether when the experiences of the soul take a particular form, such as visions, sensations, etc., the which, as they are generally received under some visible representation, may, then, be described by this or some other semblance wherein the sense participates. But this power of expression does not apply to pure contemplation; for this is inexpressible and may scarce be spoken of, wherefore it is called secret.

And not only for this reason, is it called, and *is* secret, but, likewise, because a peculiar feature of this Mystic Wisdom is, that it hides [and shrouds] the soul within itself. For, apart from its more usual manifestations, it sometimes absorbs and gathers up the soul into its secret abyss, after such a manner that she distinctly perceives herself rapt away to an immeasurable distance and remoteness from all created things; so that she sees herself, as it were, set in a profound and unfathomable solitude—an immense and boundless desert—where no mortal foot may tread; as delightful, sweet, and amorous as it is profound, unending and lonely, where the soul, in like proportion as she soars above all temporal beings, finds herself hidden and in inviolable secrecy. And to such an extent doth this Abyss of Wisdom elevate and ennoble the soul, she being plunged into the innermost recesses of the science of love, that not only doth it make her to know that all mortal conditions are infinitely mean and abject in respect of this supreme knowledge and Divine cognition, but likewise enables her to see how weak and meaningless, and, after a manner, utterly unsuitable are all speech and words which we apply in this life to Divine things, and that it is impossible by any human mode and way, be our words as sublime, lofty and pregnant as they may, to know and conceive of them as they are, save by the direct Illumination of this Mystic Theology. Therefore, when the soul perceives by its radiance, this truth, that it is not to be fathomed, much less expressed by any human or ordinary language, she rightly calls it secret. This property of being secret and hidden, and absolutely above the comprehension of the human intellect, which is an essential peculiarity of this Divine Contemplation, arises not only from its supernatural nature, but from its being a guide, a guide to lead the soul to the perfections of the Union with God; the which perfections, in so far as they are not to be humanly comprehended, we must pursue our journey towards them bereft of knowledge, and divinely ignorant. For, to speak mystically, as we are doing, we cannot know nor grasp the nature of these things, so long as we go about seeking for them, only when we have found and tried them. For, says the prophet Baruch, speaking of this Divine Wisdom: *Non est qui possit scire vias ejus, neque qui exquirat semitas ejus.*[66] None may understand His ways, nor none imagine His paths. Likewise the Royal prophet, conversing with God of this journey of the soul, gives utterance as follows: *Illuxerunt coruscationes tuæ orbi terrae: commota est, et contremuit terra: in mari via tua, et semitæ tuæ in aquis multis: et vestigia tua non cognoscentur.*[67] Thy splendor shone forth, and lit up the utmost ends of the earth, the earth was moved and trembled: Thy road is in the sea, and Thy paths in deep waters, and Thy footsteps shall not be known. All which, speaking spiritually, is understood to mean what we are saying. For the lighting up of the ends of the earth by the luster of God, is the enlightenment of the powers of the soul by this Divine contemplation; and for the earth to quake and be affrighted, is the grievous purgation it effects upon her. And to say that the road of God, which the soul pursues on her journey towards Him, lies in the sea, and His footsteps in deep waters, wherefore they shall not be known, means that this journey towards God is as secret and hidden from the sense of the soul as is the road He takes through the sea, whose paths and footsteps are unknown, to the physical sense of the body. For this is the property of the steps and footfalls that God imprints upon those souls He deigns to draw unto Himself, making them great in the union of His Wisdom, that they are not heard. For which reason, we find these words in the book of Job, where he lays stress upon this matter: *Numquid nosti semitas nubium magnas, et perfectas scientias?*[68] Peradventure hast thou known the paths of the monstrous clouds, or perfect knowledge. Meaning by this the ways and roads whereby God aggrandizes souls and perfects them in His wisdom, the which are here meant by clouds. The result, then, is that this contemplation which leads the soul upward to God, is Secret Wisdom.

IT IS SHEWN HOW THIS SECRET WISDOM IS ALSO A STAIR

It remains to be seen in the second place, to wit, how this Secret Wisdom is also a stair. As to which we must know, that for many reasons may this Secret Contemplation be called a stair. For, like as a fortress is stormed by a stair or ladder, and the valuables and possessions stored therein fall into the hands of the besiegers, so, also, by this Secret Contemplation (although she knows not how), the soul mounts aloft, and scales, rung by rung, to the heights and knowledge and possession of the wealth and treasures of Heaven.

The which the Royal Prophet David well expresses when he says: *Beatus vir, cujus est auxilium ab te: ascensiones in corde suo disposuit, in valle lacrymarum in loco, quem posuit. Etenim benedictionem dabit legislator, ibunt de virtue in virtutem; videbitur Deus Deorum in Sion.*[69] Blessed is he who possesses Thy help and favor, for in the heart of such a one He has placed His ascendings in the valley of tears in the place He appointed; for after this manner shall the Lord of Judgment give His benediction, and they shall climb from virtue to virtue as from step to step, and the God of Gods shall be seen in Sion, the which are the treasures of the fortress of Sion, which is blessedness.

We may, likewise, call it a stair or ladder, for just as we make use of the rungs of a ladder not only to mount but to descend; so, also, these same communications made to the soul by this Secret Contemplation, whereby she mounts to God, abases her in herself. For those communications which are, in very sooth, from God, possess this property, that at one and the same time they humble and exalt her. For, on this road, to descend is to mount, and to mount is to descend, for here, he who humbles himself is exalted, and he who exalts himself is humbled: *Qui se exaltat, humiliabatur, et qui se humiliat, exaltabitur.*[70] And, setting aside the fact that the virtue of humility is most noble, God, so as to exercise the soul therein, makes her to climb this ladder, to bring her down, and brings her down to raise her. So that, thus may be accomplished the saying of the Wise One: *Antequam conteratur, exaltatur cor hominis: et antequam glorificetur humilitur.*[71] Before the soul shall be exalted, she shall be humbled; and before she shall be humbled, she shall be exalted. Likewise, in consonance with this property of the ladder, the soul that is fain to reflect thereon shall most clearly perceive (apart from its spiritual significance, which she doth not realize), how many are the ups and downs she suffers on this journey, and how the fair weather she enjoys is soon followed by some storm and trial: to such an extent, that it seems as if the calm was only sent her in order to prepare and strengthen her for her present suffering; as, likewise, after misery and torment comes abundance and serenity. So that, to the soul it seems that of express purpose she was first set in this austere vigil, to prepare her for the high Festival that followed. And this is the usual style and method of the state of Contemplation, that until the soul reaches the state of perfect quiet she is never stable in one condition, but is ever rising and descending. The reason for this is that, as the state of perfection, which consists in the perfect love of God and contempt of oneself, cannot exist without these two parts, which are the knowledge of God and of ourselves, and that, of necessity, the soul must first be practiced in the one and then the other, being given to taste of the one by being exalted, and being made the other by being humiliated, until having acquired the habits of perfection, she, at last, ceases to mount and to descend; having now reached to and united herself with God, who crowns the summit of this ladder and on whom it rests and is supported. Because this ladder of contemplation, which as we have said, emanates from God, is figured forth by the ladder seen by Jacob whilst he slept, up and down which the angels of God mounted and descended, from God to man and from man to God, on whom its apex rested: *Angelos quoque Dei ascendentes, et descendentes per eam, et Dominum innixum scalæ.*[72] All which, the Divine Scripture saith, took place by night whilst Jacob slept, to shew how secret and unlike from all man's knowledge is this road and ascension to God. The which is, indeed, evident, since, as a rule, that which it contains of greatest value (which is, the loss and annihilation of himself), he counts as worthless, and that which is least worth (which is the achievement of his own comfort and pleasure, wherein he more often loses than gains), that he sets most store by.

But, now to speak somewhat more substantially and particularly of this ladder of secret contemplation, we shall say that the chief property wherefore it is here called a ladder, is because Contemplation is the Science of Love, which is an infused and amorous apprehension of God, and which gradually enlightens and impassions the soul, until it elevates her step by step, to God her Maker. For love alone it is that unites and joins the soul with God. Wherefore, in order to make this still clearer, we shall here proceed to set down the steps of this Divine ladder, briefly describing the signatures[73] and effects of each one, in order that the soul may thereby conjecture in which of them she is, and to this end, we shall classify them according to their effects, as do St. Bernard and St. Thomas; and because the knowledge of them in themselves (forasmuch as this ladder of love is so secret, that God alone can measure and weigh it in the scales) is not possible by any human way.

WHEREIN IS COMMENCED THE INTERPRETATION OF THE TEN STEPS
(DEGREES) OF THE MYSTICAL STAIR OF DIVINE LOVE AS SET FORTH BY
ST. BERNARD AND ST. THOMAS: WE BEGIN WITH THE FIRST FIVE

We say, then, that the steps of this ladder of love which the soul climbs, one by one, in her ascension to God, are ten. The first degree of love makes the soul most beneficially sicken and languish. It is of this grade of love that the Spouse speaks, when she says: *Adjuro vos, filiæ Jerusalem, si inveneritis dilectum meum, ut nuncietis ei, quia amore langueo.*[74] I adjure ye, oh daughters of Jerusalem! That if ye meet with my Belovèd, ye shall say to him that I am sick for love. But this sickness is not mortal, only for the glory of God, for, therein is the soul deprived of all strength to sin and of all things that are not God, for God's own sake, as David testifies saying: *Defecit spiritus meus.*[75] My soul is brought low, that is, as to all things to thy health, like as he says in another place: *Deficit in salutare tuum anima mea.*[76] For, in like manner as the sick man first loses all appetite and relish for food and changes hue, so, likewise, in this grade of love, the soul loses her relish and appetite for all things, and changes color like a lover. The soul doth not fall into this sickness, unless the excess of heat be sent to her from above, which is, in this state, the mystical fever, as is shewn by this verse of David, which says: *Pluviam voluntariam segregabis, Deus, hæriditati tuæ, et infirmata est: tu verò perfecisti eam.*[77] This sickness and languishing from all things, which is the first grade and step of going to God, we have well set forth above, when we described the extinction wherein the soul sees herself, when she starts to climb the first rungs of this ladder of Contemplative Purgation, when she can find no support, relish, comfort, nor rest for the sole of her foot, in any living thing. Wherefore, from this grade, she soon begins to scale the others.

The second grade forces the soul to seek for God without ceasing. Whence, the Bride says that, as she sought for him by night within her bed (whereon according to the first grade of love she lay weak and fainting and found him not), she cried: *Surgam, et quæram queam diligit anima mea.*[78] I will arise, and seek Him who loves my soul. The which, as we say, the soul does ceaselessly, as David admonishes in these words: *Quærite Dominum . . . quærite faciem ejus semper.*[79] Seek the face of God always, and seeking Him in all things, fix thy mind on none, until thou shalt have found Him. Like as the Bride, who, when she had asked about Him of the guards, at once passed on and left them.

And likewise, Mary Magdalene, who did not so much as cast a look at the angels round the sepulchre. Here, in this grade, the soul goeth with such solicitude, that in everything she seeks for her Belovèd; in all her thoughts is she stricken with the thought of the Beloved One: in all her words, in all her actions, in whatsoever business she is about, she must, at once, speak and discourse of her Belovèd; when she eats, when she sleeps, when she keeps vigil, when she busies herself in any matter, all her heart is full of her Belovèd, as has been said above, in the description of the longings of love. Then, when at length her love begins to recover from its sickness and to gather strength in this second grade, she, at once, begins to climb the third, by means of some degree of fresh purgation in this night, as we shall afterwards state, the which produces on the soul the following effects.

The third step of the amorous ladder is that which forces the soul to action, and inspires her with vital heat so that she may not falter. Of this says the Royal prophet: *Beatus vir, qui timet Dominum: in mandatis ejus volet nimis.*[80] Blessed is the man who fears the Lord, for all his desire is set on performing His commandments. Whence, if fear, inasmuch as it is a child of love, produces this effect of greed, what shall love itself do? In this grade the utmost she can do for the Belovèd the soul counts as nought, her manifold deeds as few, the length of time devoted by her to His service as a moment, because of this burning furnace of love wherein she is consumed. Like Jacob, to whom the seven years over and above the other seven he was forced to serve, seemed few by reason of the greatness of his love: *Servivit ergo Jacob pro Rachel septem annis, et videbantur illi pauci dies præ amoris magnitudine.*[81] Now if the love of Jacob which was only human could effect so much, what shall not that of the Creator do, when, in this third grade, it seizes upon the soul? Here, the soul, by reason of the great love she bears to God, is deeply afflicted and in anguish for the little she does for Him; and if it were permitted her to tear herself into a thousand shreds for His sake, she would be consoled. Therefore she accounts herself for useless in all she does, and it seems to her she lives in vain. And hence, springs up in her another admirable effect, which is, that she is absolutely convinced that, in very sooth, her wickedness is greater than that of every other soul put together. First, because love teaches her the immensity of God's deserving; and secondly, though the deeds she now performs for the sake of God are many, she yet realizes the full extent of their imperfections and defects, and each one of them fills her with grief and confusion, because she knows how unspeakably mean and base is her performance in respect of so great a Lord. In this third grade, the soul is very far from harboring vain-glory or presumption, or condemning others. These are the solicitous effects, together with many others of a like nature, which this third grade of love produces on the soul; and by reason thereof, the soul in it, gathers strength and courage to mount to the fourth which follows.

The fourth grade of this ladder of love is that which produces in the soul, a constant and steadfast and unwearying endurance. For, as says St. Augustine, the greatest, gravest, most weighty and ponderous matters, love counts as nothing and makes light of. It was of this grade that the Bride spoke, when, at length, desiring to see herself in the supreme and last one of all, she said to the Spouse: *Pone me ut signaculum super cor tuum, ut signaculum super brachium tuum: quia fortis est ut mors dilectio; dura sicut infernus æmulatio.* Place me as a sign upon thy heart, and as a sign about thy arm: for delight, that is, the act and work of love, is strong as death, and rivalry, obstinate and enduring as hell. In this grade the spirit acquires such strength that so denominates the flesh and holds it in as little, as the tree one of its countless leaves. Here, the soul, in no way, seeks her own comfort and pleasure, neither in God nor in any other thing, nor doth she, from any motive of self interest or of consolation for herself, beseech the favor of God. For, now, all her care is, as to how she may please and serve Him in some-what, for the sake of what is due to Him and that she has received from Him, cost her what it may. She cries within her heart and spirit: Alas my God and my Lord! How many are there who go about to seek in Thee their own comfort and delight, and to whom Thou concedest mercies and gifts; but they who endeavor to please Thee and give Thee some-what at their cost, postponing all desires of their own, are exceeding few; for, it is not from any lack of will in Thee, my God, to shower on us Thy favors: it is we who fall short, by not devoting those we have received, to Thy service, so as to force Thee to bestow them on us constantly. This grade of love is exceeding lofty; for, as in it, the soul ever follows after God, with passionate love and longing to suffer for Him, His Majesty, ofttimes, and very frequently, gladdens and rejoices her by the fulness of delight, visiting her in the spirit most sweetly and deliciously; because the immense love of the Verb Christ may not suffer the pangs of His lover without coming to her rescue. The which He affirmed by Jeremiah, saying: *Recordatus sum tui, miserans adolescentiam tuam . . . quando secuta es me in deserto.*[82] I have remembered thee, and have had compassion on thy youth and tender years, when thou followedest me in the desert, which to speak spiritually, is the lack of support in all created things, which, in this grade, the soul feels interiorly, finding no stay nor rest in anything. This fourth grade inflames the soul after such a fashion, and kindles in her so fierce a desire for God, that it brings her to climb the fifth, which is that which follows.

The fifth grade of this ladder of love forces the soul to hunger and crave ardently for God without rest or ceasing. In this grade, such is the vehemence that the lover feels to seize upon the Belovèd and be united with Him, that any delay, however slight, becomes to her most wearisome, unendurable, unending, and oppressive, and always does she think that she is on the point of seizing Him in her arms; and when she sees her desire frustrated (which is almost at every step) her eagerness weakens, as saith the Psalmist when speaking of this grade: *Concupiscit, et deficit anima mea in atria Domini.*[83] My soul longeth and fainteth in the dwellings of the Lord. In this grade the lover must either possess that she loves or die, like as Rachel, for the great longing she had for children, said to Jacob her husband: *De mihi liberos, alioquin moriar.*[84] Give me sons: if not, I die. Here, the soul waxes fat on love; for so as was her hunger is her abundance; after such sort that, hence, she may now mount to the sixth grade, which produces the effects which follow.

WHEREIN ARE SET DOWN THE REMAINING FIVE GRADES OF LOVE

The sixth grade makes the soul to fleet swiftly towards God. And so fleets her hope without stopping to draw breath: for, in this grade, the love which has fortified her makes her to fly with the swiftness of light. Of the which grade, Isaiah also saith: *Qui autem sperant in Domino, mutabunt fortitudinem, assument pennas sicut aquilæ current, et non laborabunt, ambulabunt, et non deficient.*[85] The saints that wait on God shall change strength, they shall take wings like to the eagle, they shall fly, and not wax weak. These words, likewise, of the Psalm also apply to this grade: *Quemadmodum desiderat cervus ad fontes aquarum: ita desiderat anima mea ad te, Deus.*[86] For like as the hart desireth the water brooks, my soul longeth after Thee, my God. The reason of this swiftness of love which the soul acquires in this grade is that, now her charity is boundless, and that she herself is almost, if not entirely purified, as the Psalm saith: *Sine iniquitate cucurri.*[87] And in another Psalm: *Viam mandatorum tuorum cucurri, cùm dilatasti cor meum.*[88] I ran forward upon the road of Thy commandments when Thou broadenedst out my heart; and so, from this sixth grade, she is soon placed in the seventh, which is as follows.

The seventh grade of this ladder makes the soul most vehemently to dare, with which intense and amorous impetus she is so carried away, that she neither listens to judgment which would bid her wait, nor heeds the counsel that might check her course, nor can shame itself restrain her; because the favor that God now showers upon the soul, makes her violent and forward. Whence follows what saith the Apostle, and it is this: that charity believeth all things, hopeth all things and can do all things: *Omnia credit, omnia sperat omnia sustinet.*[89] It was of this grade that Moses spoke when he asked God to spare his people, and if not, to blot his name from out of the book of life wherein He had written it: *Aut dimitte eis hanc noxam, aut si non facis, dele me de libro tuo, quem scripsisti.*[90] These souls get from God what with delight they ask of him. Whence says David: *Delectare in Domino: et dabit tibi petitiones cordis tui.*[91] Delight thyself in God, and He shall give thee the petitions of thy heart. It was in this degree that the Spouse waxed bold and said: *Osculatur me osculo oris sui.*[92] But here it is most important to observe that it is not permissible to the soul to wax daring, if she feels not the interior favor of the scepter of God inclined towards her; lest, perchance, she fall not from the other grades which she has, until then scaled, in the which she must always guard herself with great humility. From this daring and command God gives to the soul in this seventh grade to wax bold with Him from sheer vehemence of love follows the eighth, which is when she seizes upon her Belovèd and makes herself one with Him.

The eighth grade of love makes the soul to seize upon and press Him in her arms, never loosening her grasp according to what the

Bride says after the following manner: *Inveni, quam diligit anima mea: tenui eum, nec dimittam.*[93] I found Him who loves my heart and life, I held Him, and I will not loose Him. In this grade of love the soul satisfies her desire, but not without intermission, for some place their foot on this rung and then withdraw it; for, were it otherwise, and they remained in this grade, they would enter into the possession of a certain glory even in this life, and therefore, the soul spends but a short space therein. For, to the prophet Daniel, as he was a man of big desires, it was told to him from God that he should remain in this grade: *Daniel vir desideriorum . . . sta in gradu tuo.*[94] From this grade proceeds the ninth, which belongs to those who have reached perfection, as we shall say.

The ninth degree of love makes the soul to burn with exceeding softness. This degree is the state of the perfect, who, at last, burn sweetly in God. For this soft and delicious fire and ardor is caused in them by the Holy Spirit by reason of the union they have with God. Wherefore, saith St. Gregory, speaking of the Apostles, when the Holy Ghost descended visibly upon them, they burnt interiorly and softly in love. No man may speak of the gifts and riches of God which the soul enjoys in this grade; for if many books were multiplied concerning it, the greater part would still be left unsaid. Whereof I say no more, save that from this follows the tenth and last grade of this ladder of love, which no longer pertains to this life.

The tenth and last grade of this ladder of love makes the soul to be entirely assimilated to God, by reason of the lucid vision of God which she then possesses, for having even in this life arrived at the ninth grade, she leaves the flesh. And in the case of these, for they are few, love is wont to accomplish, having thoroughly purged and scourged them in this life, what on others Purgatory effects in the next. Whence St. Matthew says: *Beati mundo corde: quoniam ipsi Deum videbunt.*[95] And, as we say, this insight is the cause of the entire similitude of the soul with God, for so saith St. John: *Scimus quoniam cùm apparuerit, similes ei erimus: quoniam videbimus eum sicuti est.*[96] We know that we shall be like unto Him, for we shall see Him as He is. Where all that constitutes the soul shall be like to God; for which reason, she shall be called, and shall be, God by participation. This is the secret staircase the soul

speaks of here, although, already, in these higher grades, it is far from
being secret from her, for, much is revealed to her by love in the great
effects it works upon her. But on this last grade of clear vision, which
is the last rung of the ladder which rests on God, as we have said, no
longer is there anything hidden from the soul, by reason of her total
assimilation. Whence our Savior says: *Et in illo die me non rogabitis
quidquam.*[97] In that day thou shalt enquire of me nothing, for, until
that day, to whatever heights the soul may soar, somewhat remains
hidden from her, and in like proportion to that which still lacks of
absolute assimilation with the Divine essence. In this way, by this
Mystical Theology and Secret Love doth the soul go, going forth from
all things and from herself, and mounting to God. For love is like to
fire, which ever leaps upwards, with desire to be engulfed in the center
of its sphere.

WHEREIN THE MEANING OF THIS WORD "DISGUISED," AND THE MASQUERADING
COLORS OF THE SOUL IN THIS NIGHT ARE DECLARED AND DISPLAYED

It now remains, then, after we have set forth the reasons wherefore the
soul called this contemplation: "The Secret Stairway" also, to state as
to the third word of the line, to wit "disguised," why the soul says that
she set forth by this "Secret Stair disguised." For the fuller understanding thereof, it is essential to know that, to disguise oneself is the
same as to dissemble and hide oneself under some other dress and
appearance than our own; either that we may under this guise or
semblance make manifest the desires and pretensions we harbor in
our hearts, so that we may win the favor and affection of one we dearly
love; or that we may the better conceal ourselves from our rivals, and
thus forward the end we have in view.

And in such circumstances, we choose such a dress and livery as
may best represent and shadow forth the affection of our heart, and
disguise ourselves more safely from our enemies. So with the soul,
who, now alight with love of her Spouse Christ, to the end that she
may captivate His favor, and conquer His affection, sets forth disguised
in that travesty which most vividly represents the desires of her spirit,
and most suited to secure her a fair and prosperous journey, safe from

the attacks of her adversaries and enemies, which are the World, the Flesh, and the devil. And to this end the livery she wears, is made up of three chief colors, which are, white, green, and red: which denote the three theological virtues, which are, Faith, Hope, and Charity, wherewith she shall not only win the favor and inclination of her Belovèd, but shall walk protected and secure from her three enemies: for Faith is an inner tunic of so fine a whiteness, that it completely deprives the mind of sight. And so when the soul sets forth upon her journey, being clothed with Faith, the devil sees her not, nor succeeds in checking her, for, under the great defense of Faith, she goeth in safety from the devil, who is her most powerful and astute enemy.

Wherefore, St. Peter found no greater defense than Faith, whereby to escape his clutches, when he said: *Cui resistite fortes in Fide*.[98] And if she would secure the favor of, and union with, the Beloved, she can clothe herself with no better tunic and inner shift, to be the basis and groundwork of all the other garments of virtue, than this whiteness of Faith, for without it, as saith the Apostle, it is impossible to please God: *Sine Fide autem impossible est placere Deo*.[99] And with Faith, if it is lively and vital she pleases Him, and appears comely in His eyes: *Sponsabo te mihi in Fide*,[100] which is as much as to say, If thou wilt, oh soul, unite and wed with me, thou must come clothed interiorly with Faith.

This whiteness of Faith the soul wears when she sallies forth into this dark night, and she journeys (as we have said above) in darkness and interior conflict, deprived of all comfort of intellectual light, as well as celestial, since the sky seems shut to her, and God is hiding; nor yet does she find it from below, since those who instructed her satisfied her not, yet still she bore it all with constancy and persevered, and passing through these trials without losing heart or allowing her confidence to be shaken in her Belovèd; He, who in trials and tribulations proves the Faith of His Spouse, after such sort that she may afterwards acclaim, in all truth, in the words of David: *Propter verba labiorum tuorum ego custodivi vias duras*.[101] By reason of the words of thy lips, I was held to hard roads.

Then above all this white tunic of Faith, the soul now invests herself with the second color, which is a garment of green. By which color is signified the virtue of Hope, wherewith, first of all, the soul delivers and defends herself from her second enemy, which is the World. For this lively green of living hope in God gives to the soul, such vitality, and courage, and such a soaring upwards to the things of life eternal, that, in comparison with what she hopes for there, all worldly things seem to her (as is indeed the truth), dry, withered, dead, and of no account. Now she strips and despoils herself of all the garments and vestures of the world, nor setting her heart on, nor hoping for ought there is, or is to be, therein, living solely clad in the hope of life eternal. Wherefore, her heart being so exalted above the world, not only can it nor touch, nor seize, nor even turn to watch her in her flight. And so with this green livery and disguise the soul goes most secure from her second enemy, which is the World. For, as to Hope, St. Paul calls it The Helmet of Safety: *Galeam Spem Salutis:*[102] which is a piece of armor to protect the whole head, and cover it, in such sort, that no part thereof remains open save a vizor for the eyes. And this same property hath Hope, for she envelops all the organs of the head and of the heart; so that they cannot be engulfed in anything of the world, nor leaves a loophole whereby some arrow from the world may wound them; one vizor alone she leaves, so that the eyes may direct their gaze upwards, and no more, for Hope's usual office in the soul, is solely to raise the eyes to look at God alone, as says David: *Oculi mei Semper ad Dominum.*[103] Hoping for nothing good from any other direction, save, as he says in another Psalm: *Sicut oculi ancillæ in manibus dominæ suæ: ita oculi nostri ad Dominum Deum nostrum, donec misereatur nostri.*[104] Like as the eyes of the handmaiden are fixed upon the hands of her mistress, so are ours on our Lord God, until he shall take compassion upon us, who wait on Him.

In this green livery (forasmuch as the soul ever keeps her eyes turned towards God, and heeds nought else save Him), the Belovèd takes such delight that it is truth to say He is fain to give the soul all she hopes for. Therefore He says to her in the Canticles, that one glance from her eye wounded Him to the heart: *Vulnerasti cor meum in uno oculorum tuorum.*[105] Without this green livery of absolute hope in God, the soul could not have gone forth on this, her quest of love,

for she might achieve nought; forasmuch as it is stubborn and irresistible Hope which impels her on, and wins the victory.

In this livery of Hope the soul walks disguised through this secret
and obscure night; for she goes so emptied out of all stays and belongings, that her eyes and anxiety are fixed on nothing else, save God,
abasing her mouth to the dust, if, peradventure, Hope is only by her
side, as we have quoted before from Jeremiah.

Over the white and the green, for the final touch and ornament of
this disguise and livery, the soul now wears the third color, which is a
lovely mantle of scarlet. Whereby is denoted the third Virtue, which is
Charity, wherewith, not only are the other two colors made more
gracious, but the soul is made to soar so high, that she is placed very
near to God, in so beautiful and lovely a seeming, that she is emboldened to exclaim: *Nigra sum, sed formosa, filiæ Jerusalem: ideò delexit me
Rex, et introduxit me in Cubiculum suum.*[106] Though I be black, oh ye
daughters of Jerusalem! Yet I am comely; therefore the King hath
loved me, and hath placed me in his bed. With this livery of charity
which is that of love, not only doth the soul defend and hide herself
from her third enemy, which is the Flesh (for where there is unfeigned
love of God, love of self and self's belongings cannot enter in), but
even gives validity and resistance to the other virtues, giving them
strength and vigor to protect the soul, and grace and elegance to
delight therewith the Belovèd One; for without charity, no virtue is
gracious before God. For this is the crimson spoken of in the
Canticles, whereby we ascend to the couch whereon reposes God,
Reclinatorium aureum, ascensum purpureum.[107] In this crimson livery the
soul walks clad, when (as has been above declared in the first Song)
she goes forth out of herself into the obscure night, far from all
created things, "With longing flaming into love," by this secret stair of
contemplation, to the perfect union of love with God, He who is her
Belovèd Health and Savior.

This, then, is the disguise which the soul saith she wears in the
night of Faith and on this secret stair; and these are the three colors
thereof. The which are a most yielding disposition in the soul to unite
herself with God, according to her three faculties, which are Memory,
Intellect, and Will. For Faith voids and darkens the intellect of all its

human knowledge, and, by so doing, prepares it for union with the Divine Wisdom. And Hope empties and alienates the memory from all creature possessions; for, as says St. Paul, Hope is for that we do not possess. *Spes autem, quæ videtur, non est spes.*[108] And therefore, it alienates the memory from all possible possessions in this life, and sets it upon what it hopes to enjoy in the future. And this is why the hope of God alone, can absolutely dispose the memory because of the vacuum it causes therein, to be united with him. Just in the same way doth charity void and empty the affections and appetites of the will of whatsoever thing that is not God, and sets them on Him alone; and so this virtue prepares this faculty and unites it with God through love. Whence, as the office of these virtues is to alienate the soul from all that is less than God, they consequently possess that of joining her with Him. And so, unless she travels invested, in very truth, with the raiment of these virtues, it is impossible to arrive at the perfection of love with God. Whence, if the soul would achieve her purpose, which was the amorous and most sweet union with her Belovèd, it was most necessary and fitting for her to assume this garb and vesture. And likewise her success in donning and persevering therein, until she achieved the end and purpose she so ardently desired, which was the union of love, was most exceeding good fortune; wherefore the line following says thus:

WHEREIN IS INTERPRETED THE THIRD LINE OF THE SECOND SONG

OH GLADSOME HAP

It is exceeding clear that it was indeed a blissful chance for the soul to start forth upon such an enterprise as this, wherein she delivered herself from the devil, and the world, and from her own sensuality; and having achieved the liberty of spirit precious and desired of all, went from the lower to the higher, from earthly, made herself Celestial, from human, Divine, coming at last, to have all her converse in Heaven, as happens in this state of perfection, as we shall go on to shew, although, now, with somewhat more brevity; since those matters of most importance (and the end that I mainly proposed to myself in this matter, was to explain this night to many souls who pass through it, and were ignorant thereof, as is stated in the prologue) have been already adequately declared and set forth (although falling far short of the reality) how great the riches are it brings along with it to the soul, and what a blissful chance it is for him who wins therethrough, so that when they shall shrink with horror from such poignant trials, they may take courage, in the certain hope of the innumerable and incomparable gifts as are therein achieved. And likewise, besides this, it was indeed a happy chance for the soul, in respect of what she goes on to say in the following line.

THE FOURTH LINE IS EXPOUNDED. THE MARVELOUS HIDING PLACE
WHEREIN THE SOUL IS BESTOWED IN THIS NIGHT IS DESCRIBED, AND HOW,
ALTHOUGH THE DEVIL HATH ENTRY INTO OTHER GRADES OF GREAT
EXCELSITUDE, HE CANNOT ENTER INTO THIS

IN DARKNESS AND IN SECRET I CREPT FORTH

"Encelada" is as much as to say: in hiding or in concealment; and, therefore, that the soul says here, that she set forth "In darkness, and in hiding," is the more fully to shew us the great safety she has spoken of in the first line of this song, wherewith, by means of this obscure contemplation, she goes forth on her journey to the union of Love with God.

For the soul, then, to say: "In darkness, and in hiding," means that, inasmuch as she went in darkness after the fashion described, she journeyed hidden and concealed from the devil, and safe from his guiles and ambushes. The reason why the soul goes freed and hidden from the snares of the devil, is because the infused contemplation which now guides her, is instilled into her passively and secretly, in the darkness of the senses and the interior and exterior powers of the sensitive part. And hence it is, that not only does she go free and concealed from the impediment which these two powers may interpose in respect of her physical nature and weakness, but also from the lyings in wait of the devil who, unless by means of these faculties of the sensitive part can neither grasp nor know that which is in the soul, and passes within her. Whence, the more spiritual, interior, and remote from the senses is her communication with God, so much the less does the devil succeed in apprehending it. And so, it is of the utmost importance for the safety of the Soul, that her interior converse with God should be in such a sort, that the senses of the inferior part themselves, be left in darkness and ignorance, and not perceive it. First, so as to give place for a greater abundance of the spiritual communication, the liberty of the spirit not being hindered by the weakness of the sensitive part. The second, because the soul goes more securely, the devil being powerless to reach her inmost recesses. And to this purpose may we understand this text of the Savior, speaking spiritually, to wit: *Nesciat sinistra tua quid faciat dextera tua.*[109] Let not thy left hand know what thy right hand doeth. Which is as much as to say: let not what passeth in the right, which is the higher and spiritual part of the soul, be known of the left; that is, let it be after such a sort that the lower portion of thy soul, which is the sensitive part, apprehend it not; let it be secret between the spirit and God alone. It is, indeed, true that very often these spiritual communications are profoundly impressed on the most interior and secret parts of the soul, although the devil cannot come at what and how they are, yet, by reason of the great hush and silence which fall upon the senses and faculties of the sensitive part, which certain of them produce, he sees that they are there, and that the soul is in the act of receiving some great favor. And, then, since he perceives that he cannot reach to the bottom of the soul to oppose them, he does his best to startle and perturb the sensitive part, where he *can* reach, now with pain, now with terror and dread, with intent, by this means, to trouble and disturb the higher and spiritual part of the soul, in respect of this favor which she then receives and enjoys. But ofttimes, when the communication of such contemplation seizes upon the spirit absolutely, and overpowers it, his diligence to disquieten her, avails him nothing, nay rather, then, doth the soul receive fresh benefits, love, and a securer peace; for, when she feels the perturbing presence of her enemy, oh, most wonderful thing! And although she knows not how it happens, she enters still deeper into the secret recesses of her own interior, perceiving, indeed, that she bestows herself in a most sure refuge, where she is at a greater distance and more surely hidden from the enemy; and thus the peace and joy that the devil aimed to rob her of are abundantly increased. And then all her former fear falls away, and she knows clearly that she is free, and sings with joy to see herself in such serene and tranquil peace, rejoicing in the tenderness and savor of the Spouse in so hidden a refuge that neither world nor devil can give or take away. The soul, therein, perceiving the truth of that spoken by the Spouse in respect of the same matter in the Canticles: *En lectulum Salomonis sexaginta fortes ambiunt . . . propter timores nocturnos.*[110] Behold sixty armed men surround the bed of Solomon, on account of the terrors of the night. And this strength and peace she tastes, although she often feels her flesh and bones tormented from without. At other times, when she shares the spiritual communication with the senses, the devil may more easily succeed by means of the senses in troubling and startling the spirit with these terrors. And then the torment and woe he causes in the spirit are exceeding great, and ofttimes beyond the power of words to describe; for as the struggle is between spirit and spirit, the horror caused by the evil spirit in the good, I mean in the soul, when his tumultuous influence reaches her, is intolerable. The which, also, the Spouse in the Canticles refers to, when she says that happened to her in like manner, at the time she was fain to descend into the interior folding inwards of the soul to enjoy these graces, saying: *Descendi in hortum nucum, ut viderem poma convallium, et inspicerem, si floruisset vinea . . . nescivi: anima mea conturbavit me propter quadrigas Aminadab.*[111] I went down to the garden of the nuts to see the apples of the valleys, and if the vines had blossomed; I swooned, my soul was troubled by the chariots of Aminadab, which is the devil.

At other times, this contradiction of the devil takes place when God bestows mercies on the soul through the guardian angel, for these, sometimes, the devil succeeds in perceiving, for God doth, as a rule, allow them to be discerned by the adversary. First, so that He may work His utmost against them in accordance with the scales of justice, that, therefore, the devil may not allege his right, saying that he is given no opportunity to make conquest of the soul, as he did of Job. And, so, it is fitting that God should clear the lists, so that the two combatants may meet on more equal terms, to wit, the good angel and the bad in their struggle for the soul; so that the victory may be more notorious and glorious, and the soul victorious and faithful in temptation, be more signally rewarded.

Here it is proper to note that this is the reason why, sometimes, in this order which God sets Himself in His conduct of the soul, He gives the devil leave to trouble and to tempt her: like as, when she receives visions through the good angel, God also allows the bad angel to put before her false visions of the selfsame kind; after such sort, that if the soul be not wary, so alike are they in seeming, she may easily be deceived, as have been many in this way.

Whereof there is an example in Exodus, where is said that all the true signs made by Moses were falsely reproduced by the magicians of Pharaoh. For if he evoked frogs, they also evoked them; if he turned water into blood, they did so likewise. Nor does Satan content himself with imitating this sort of corporal visions alone, but also adventures on the spiritual communications which come through the good angel, if he chances to behold them; for, as Job hath said: *Omne sublime videt;*[112] he falsifies and meddles how he can. Although these, as they are without shape or form (for it is the nature of spirit to be formless), he cannot counterfeit and shape as he can the others, which appear under a certain phantasm or material image. And so that he may least cast doubt upon them, just in the same way as they visit the soul, he shews her as best he can, his fearsome spirit (at such time as the good angel is about to impart to her some spiritual contemplation), with a certain horror stricken and spiritual perturbation, at times most grievous to her. And, then, the soul may sometimes wrest herself away quickly from his influence, before there is time for the said horror of the evil spirit to imprint itself upon her; and she folds herself within herself, being mercifully favored thereto by the spiritual favor that the good angel then bestows upon her.

At other times God permits this perturbation and horror to last some time, which, to her, is infinitely more grievous than any torment of this life could be, and the memory thereof cleaves to her afterwards, which is enough to fill her with intense woe. All this we have said passes within the soul, although she can neither produce nor dissipate this phantom or impression. But it must be here observed, that when God permits the devil thus to afflict and constrict the soul with this spiritual horror, He does so, to purify and dispose her by this spiritual vigil, for some great festival and spiritual favor which He, who never mortifies, save to give life, nor humbles save to exalt, wills to bestow upon her. The which takes place soon after; for the soul, conformably to the dark purgation she has gone through, rejoices in the sweet and tender spiritual contemplation, at times so sublime, as to transcend all speech. That we have said is to be understood in respect of God's visits to the soul by means of the good angel, at which seasons she walks not with the same absolute safety (as has been said), nor yet, so surrounded and concealed by darkness and her disguise, that the enemy may not chance upon her somewhat. But when God, of His own motion, visits her, then the said line is indeed verified; for, in total darkness and concealment from the enemy, doth she receive the spiritual favors of God. The reason is because, as His Majesty is the Supreme Lord, He dwells substantially within the soul, where no angel nor devil may draw nigh to hear what passes, nor know the intimate and secret converse which therein passes betwixt herself and God. For these Divine communications, forasmuch as the Lord makes them of His own motion, are absolutely Divine and sovereign, and are, as it were, substantial touches of Divine Union between the soul and God; in one of which, since this is the most supreme grade of prayer there is, the soul receives greater benefit than in all the rest. For these are the touches which she received, and pleaded for in the Canticles, saying: *Osculetur me osculo oris sui.*[113] For, as it is a thing that passes so close to God, where the soul with such lovesick longing is eager to approach, she prizes and desires one touch of this Divinity more than any other mercy that God bestows. Wherefore, in the Canticles, after He had showered on her many such, for which she had sung aloud His praises; still, not being satisfied, she pleads with Him for these Divine touches, crying: *Quis mihi det te fratrem meum sugentem ubera matris meæ, ut inveniam te foris, et deosculer te, et jam me nemo despiciat?*[114] Who shall give thee to me, oh my brother! That I alone shall find thee without, sucking the breasts of my mother, so that I may kiss thee with the lips of my soul, and so, none despise me nor wax bold against me? Showing us by this, that it was the communication which God bestowed her, of His own free will, in solitude, alone on the outskirts, and in darkness from all creatures; for this is meant by the words "Alone and without sucking the breasts." The which happens when the soul, at last, with liberty of spirit, the sensitive part being powerless to hinder, nor the devil, using it as an instrument to oppose, enjoys these treasures in sweetness and infinite peace. For, then, the devil shall not wax bold against her, for he cannot reach her, nor has he power to draw nigh to hear these Divine whispers in the substance of the soul by her amorous conjunction with the substance of God. To this prize, none attains save by searching purgation and nakedness and a spiritual hiding place from everything that is creature. The which is in darkness, in which hiding place the soul confirms herself in the union with God through love, and therefore, she raises up her voice and gives utterance to her gladness in the words of the said line: "In darkness and in hiding."

When it happens that these mercies are bestowed upon the soul in hiding, which is on the spirit alone, in certain of them, the soul is wont to see herself, how it is, she knows not, so far away and remote from, in respect of the higher part from the lower, that she recognizes in herself two personalities, so distinct the one from the other, as to lead her to believe that the one has no connection with the other, as it seems to her, that it is exceedingly remote and severed from the one. And, in truth, after a certain fashion so it is; for in respect of the operation that it then accomplishes, which is entirely spiritual, it has no communication with the sensitive part. After this fashion doth the soul proceed to make herself entirely spiritual; and in this hiding place, this den, this refuge of unitive contemplation, the passions and spiritual appetites are finally, each after its own fashion, made an end of, in a most superlative degree. And so, speaking of the higher portion of the soul the last line goes on to say:

WHEREIN IS BROUGHT TO A CLOSE THE EXPOSITION OF THE SECOND SONG

MY HOUSE BEING NOW AT REST

The which is as much as to say, that as the higher portion of my soul, as well as the inferior, is now at rest as regards its appetites and passions, I stole forth to the Divine union of love of God.

Forasmuch as, by means of this troublous conflict of the obscure night (as has been said), the soul is combated and purged in two ways, to wit, in respect of the sensitive part and the spiritual with their senses, faculties, and passions, in two ways, likewise in respect of these two parts sensitive and spiritual, doth the soul come at last to achieve peace and rest. And it is for this reason (as hath also been said) that she twice repeats this line in this song and the last, by reason of these two portions of the soul, the spiritual and the sensitive; the which, if they are to be enabled to set forth on their journey to the Divine union of love, must be first reformed, set in order, and silenced as to the sensitive and spiritual, like as in the state of Innocence wherein Adam first dwelt, notwithstanding that it is not entirely delivered from the temptations of the inferior part. And thus this line which, in the first song was taken to mean the repose of the inferior and sensitive part, is in this second part to be more particularly understood of the upper and spiritual, wherefore she has repeated it twice.

The soul comes to achieve this rest and quiet of her spiritual house, habitually and perfectly (so far as this condition of our life admits of), by means of these acts, which are substantial, as it were, of the Divine union we have just spoken of, which in concealment, and hidden from the perturbations of the devil, and from her own senses and emotions, she hath received from the Divinity, wherein the soul has never ceased to purify, silence, and strengthen herself, and make herself firm and stable so as to be able, judiciously, to receive the said union, which is the Divine espousals between the soul and the Son of God. Whereupon, as soon as these two houses of the soul are both completely hushed and fortified together with all their servitors of faculties and appetites, put to sleep and in repose in respect of all things above and below, this Divine Wisdom is immediately united with the soul in a new knot of possession of love, and that which is said thereof is fulfilled: *Cum enim quietum silentium contineret omnia et nox in suo cursu medium iter haberet, omnipotens sermo tuus de cælo à regalibus sedibus prosilivit.*[115] The bride sets forth the same thing in the Canticles, saying, that after she escaped from those who stripped her of her cloak by night and sorely wounded her, she found Him whom her soul desired: *Paululum cùm pertransisem eos, invenvi, quem diligit anima mea.*[116] It is impossible to arrive at this union without great purity, and this purity is not achieved without being stripped of all created things and a lively mortification. The which is signified by the stripping off of the mantle from the Spouse and wounding her by night, when she was seeking and hunting for her Spouse; for she could not clothe herself with the new bridal robe she desired until she had cast off the old. Wherefore, he who shall refuse to set forth into this night (now described), to seek for his Belovèd and be stripped of his will and mortified, but who seeks for Him in his bed and at his ease, shall find Him not like as this soul says of herself that she found Him, when she stole forth in darkness and sick with passionate longing in her journey towards Him; inasmuch as she travels unimpeded by any obstacle of form and figure and human knowledge, which are the usual barriers between her and her lasting union with God.

The third is, that although she walks, unstayed by any special interior mental light, or exterior guide, to sustain and encourage her on this lofty road, since the darkness of this night deprives her of all such aid; still her Love and Faith which ever, like a beacon lights her way, and constantly importune her heart with thought of her Belovèd, urge and guide her forward, and make her to fleet swiftly towards her God on this lonely, solitary road, although she knows not how nor in what way.

ENDNOTES

THE DARK NIGHT OF THE SOUL AND DECLARATION OF THE SONGS

[1] Matth. vii. 14.

BOOK I

[1] Matth. vii. 3.
[2] Matth. xxv. 8.
[3] John iii. 6.
[4] 1 Cor. xiii. 6.
[5] Matth. xvi. 25, and x. 39.
[6] Apoc. iii. 8.
[7] Num. xi. 5.
[8] Can. vi. 4.
[9] Psalm lxxxiv. 9.
[10] Psalm lxxii. 21. The words used by San Juan de la Cruz are "*impureza del natural*," equivalent to the "naturals" of the old Divines: *vide* Jeremy Taylor.
[11] Psalm xlvi. 3.
[12] Matth. vii. 14.
[13] Gen. xxi. 8.
[14] Exod. iii. 5.
[15] Isaiah lviii. 10.
[16] Isaiah xxviii. 19.
[17] Isaiah xxviii. 9.
[18] Habak. ii. 1.
[19] Psalm lxii. 3.
[20] Psalm xxxviii. 3.
[21] Psalm lxxvi. 4.
[22] Psalm lxxvi. 7.
[23] San Juan's terminology will present no difficulty to the philosophical student, or to anyone conversant with the old English Divines; but it may

be as well to state that the word "sensitive" is equivalent, in more modern parlance, to "sensual," "physical," "bodily," "carnal," "fleshly."

24 Psalm l. 10.

25 Isaiah xix. 14.

26 Eccles. xxiv. 9, 10.

27 Jerem. xxxi. 81.

BOOK II

1 Spirit here is equivalent to mind or the intellectual faculty of man, although I prefer to retain the exact word used by San Juan himself.

2 Psalm cxlvii. 17.

3 Sapient ix. 15.

4 Hosea ii. 20.

5 1 Corinth. xiii. 11.

6 Eph. iv. 24.

7 Rom. xii. 2.

8 Psalm xcvi. 2.

9 Psalm xvii. 13.

10 Job vii. 20.

11 Psalm xxxviii. 12.

12 Job xxiii. 6.

13 Job xix. 21.

14 Psalm xvii. 5, 6, 7.

15 Psalm lxxxvii. 6.

16 Psalm lxxxvii. 9.

17 Jon. ii. 4.

18 Ezek. xxiv. 10.

19 Ezek. xxiv. 11.

20 Sap. iii. 6.

21 Psalm lxviii. 1.

22 Job xvi. 13.

23 Thren. iii. 4, et seq.

24 Job xii. 22.

25 Psalm cxxxviii. 12.

26 Psalm cxlii. 4.

27 Psalm xxix. 7.

28 Thren. iii. 44.

29 Ibid. No. 8.

30 Ibid. No. 8.

31 Ibid. No. 29.

32 Psalm lxxii. 22.

33 1 ad Cor. ii. 10.

34 Sap. vii. 24.

[35] 2 Cor. vi. 10.

[36] Isaiah lxiv. 4. 1 ad Cor. ii. 9.

[37] Thren. iii. 17.

[38] Psalm xxxvii. 9.

[39] Psalm xxxvii. 9.

[40] Job xxx. 16.

[41] Thren. iii. 17.

[42] Sap. vii. 11.

[43] Eccles. li. 29.

[44] Let the reader always remember that "spirit" is equivalent to the intellectual mind.

[45] Psalm lviii. 10.

[46] Deut. vi. 5.

[47] Psalm lxii. 2.

[48] Job vii. 2.

[49] Isaiah xxvi. 9.

[50] Isaiah xxvi. 9.

[51] Psalm l. 12.

[52] Thren. i. 13.

[53] Psalm cxi. 7.

[54] Eccles. li. 26.

[55] Psalm xxxviii. 4.

[56] John xx. 15.

[57] Gen. xxx. 1.

[58] Eph. i. 24.

[59] Cant. viii. 1.

[60] Matt. x. 36.

[61] Osee xiii. 9.

[62] Psalm xvii. 12.

[63] Psalm xvii. 13.

[64] Psalm xxx. 20.

[65] Acts vii. 32.

[66] Baruch iii. 31.

[67] Psalm lxxvi. 19, 20.

[68] Job xxxvii. 16.

[69] Psalm lxxxiii. 6.

[70] Luc. xiv. 11.

[71] Prov. xviii. 12.

[72] Gen. xxviii. 12.

[73] If the reader is impatient with this word, I recommend him to the perusal of the noble doctrine of the Mediæval Alchemists, and he will see how effectively, in this place, San Juan uses it.

[74] Cant. v. 8.

[75] Psalm cxlii. 7.

[76] Psalm cxviii. 81.

[77] Psalm lxvii. 10.

[78] Cant. iii. 2.

[79] Psalm civ. 4.

[80] Psalm cxi. 1.

[81] Gen. xxix. 20.

[82] Jerem. ii. 2.

[83] Psalm lxxxiii. 3.

[84] Gen. xxx. 1.

[85] Isai. xl. 31.

[86] Psalm xli. 1.

[87] Psalm lviii. 5.

[88] Psalm cxviii. 32.

[89] 1 ad Corin. xiii. 7.

[90] Exod. xxxii. 31, 32.

[91] Psalm xxxvi. 4.

[92] Cant. i. 1.

[93] Cant. iii. 4.

[94] Dan. x. 11.

[95] Matt. v. 8.

[96] 1 Joann. iii. 2.

[97] Joann. xvi. 23.

[98] 1 Peter v. 9.

[99] Hebrœor. xi. 9.

[100] Osee ii. 20.

[101] Psalm xvi. 4.

[102] Thess. v. 8.

[103] Psalm xxiv. 15.

[104] Psalm cxxii. 2.

[105] Cant. iv. 9.

[106] Cant. i. 4.

[107] Cant. iii. 10.

[108] Rom. viii. 24.

[109] Matt. vi. 3.

[110] Cant. iii. 7, 8.

[111] Cant. vi. 10.

[112] Job xli. 25.

[113] Cant. i. 1.

[114] Cant. viii. 1.

[115] Cant. iii. 4.

[116] Cant. iii. 4.

SUGGESTED READING

⊰≱⊱

BRENAN, GERALD. *St. John of the Cross: His Life and Poetry.* New York: Cambridge University Press, 1973.

CRISOGONO DE JESUS SACREMENTADO. *The Life of St. John of the Cross.* Trans. Kathleen Pond. London: Longman, Green, 1958.

DICKEN, E. W. TRUMAN. *The Crucible of Love: A Study of the Mysticism of St. Teresa of Jesus and St. John of the Cross.* New York: Sheed & Ward, 1963.

FROST, BEDE. *Saint John of the Cross.* New York: Harper & Bros., 1937.

HARDY, RICHARD. *Search for Nothing: The Life of St. John of the Cross.* New York: Crossroad, 1982.

KAVANAUGH, KIERAN, ED. *John of the Cross: Selected Writings.* New York: Paulist Press, 1987.

MERTON, THOMAS. *Contemplative Prayer.* New York: Herder & Herder, 1969.

PEERS, E. ALLISON. *Handbook to the Life and Times of St. Teresa and St. John of the Cross.* London: Burns Oates, 1954.

PEERS, E. ALLISON, TRANS. AND ED. *The Complete Works of St. John of the Cross: 3 Volumes.* Westminster, MD: Newman, 1945.

ST. TERESA OF AVILA. *The Interior Castle.* Trans. Kieran Kavanaugh. New York: Paulist Press, 1980.

WILLIAMS, ROWAN. *Christian Spirituality: A Theological History from the New Testament to Luther and St. John of the Cross.* Atlanta: John Knox Press, 1979.

Look for the following titles, available now from
The Barnes & Noble Library of Essential Reading.

Visit your Barnes & Noble bookstore,
or shop online at *www.bn.com/loer*

NONFICTION

Age of Revolution, The	Winston S. Churchill	0760768595
Alexander	Theodore Ayrault Dodge	0760773491
American Democrat, The	James Fenimore Cooper	0760761981
American Indian Stories	Zitkala-Ša	0760765502
Ancient Greek Historians, The	J. B. Bury	0760776350
Ancient History	George Rawlinson	0760773580
Antichrist, The	Friedrich Nietzsche	0760777705
Autobiography of Benjamin Franklin, The	Benjamin Franklin	0760768617
Autobiography of Charles Darwin, The	Charles Darwin	0760769087
Babylonian Life and History	E. A. Wallis Budge	0760765499
Beyond the Pleasure Principle	Sigmund Freud	0760774919
Birth of Britain, The	Winston S. Churchill	0760768579
Boots and Saddles	Elizabeth B. Custer	076077370X
Characters and Events of Roman History	Guglielmo Ferrero	0760765928
Chemical History of a Candle, The	Michael Faraday	0760765227
Civil War, The	Julius Caesar	0760768943
Common Law, The	Oliver Wendell Holmes	0760754985
Confessions	Jean-Jacques Rousseau	0760773599
Conquest of Gaul, The	Julius Caesar	0760768951
Consolation of Philosophy, The	Boethius	0760769796
Conversations with Socrates	Xenophon	0760770441

THE BARNES & NOBLE
LIBRARY OF ESSENTIAL READING

This newly developed series has been established to provide affordable access to books of literary, academic, and historic value—works of both well-known writers and those who deserve to be rediscovered. Selected and introduced by scholars and specialists with an intimate knowledge of the works, these volumes present complete, original texts in a modern, readable typeface—welcoming a new generation of readers to influential and important books of the past. With more than 100 titles already in print and more than 100 forthcoming, the Library of Essential Reading offers an unrivaled variety of thought, scholarship, and entertainment. Best of all, these handsome and durable paperbacks are priced to be exceptionally affordable. For a full list of titles, visit *www.bn.com/loer*.